P

It was only a matter of time before a clever publisher realized that there is an audience for whom *Exile on Main Street* or *Electric Ladyland* are as significant and worthy of study as *The Catcher in the Rye* or *Middlemarch* … The series … is freewheeling and eclectic, ranging from minute rock-geek analysis to idiosyncratic personal celebration — *The New York Times Book Review*

Ideal for the rock geek who thinks liner notes just aren't enough — *Rolling Stone*

One of the coolest publishing imprints on the planet — *Bookslut*

These are for the insane collectors out there who appreciate fantastic design, well-executed thinking, and things that make your house look cool. Each volume in this series takes a seminal album and breaks it down in startling minutiae. We love these. We are huge nerds — *Vice*

A brilliant series … each one a work of real love — *NME* (UK)

Passionate, obsessive, and smart — *Nylon*

Religious tracts for the rock 'n' roll faithful — *Boldtype*

[A] consistently excellent series — *Uncut* (UK)

We … aren't naive enough to think that we're your only source for reading about music (but if we had our way … watch out). For those of you who really like to know everything there is to know about an album, you'd do well to check out Continuum's "33 1/3" series of books — *Pitchfork*

For reviews of individual titles in the series, please visit our blog at 333sound.com and our website at http://www.bloomsbury.com/musicandsoundstudies

Follow us on Twitter: @333books

Like us on Facebook: https://www.facebook.com/33.3books

For a complete list of books in this series, see the back of this book

Amazing Grace

33⅓

Aaron Cohen

BLOOMSBURY ACADEMIC
NEW YORK • LONDON • OXFORD • NEW DELHI • SYDNEY

BLOOMSBURY ACADEMIC
Bloomsbury Publishing Inc
1385 Broadway, New York, NY 10018, USA
50 Bedford Square, London, WC1B 3DP, UK

BLOOMSBURY, BLOOMSBURY ACADEMIC and the Diana logo are trademarks of Bloomsbury Publishing Plc

First published in 2011 by the Continuum International Publishing Group Ltd
Reprinted by Bloomsbury Academic 2017, 2018, 2019, 2020

Cohen, Aaron.
Aretha Franklin's Amazing grace / by Aaron Cohen.
p. cm. – (33 1/3)
ISBN-13: 978-1-4411-4888-9 (pbk. : alk. paper)
ISBN-10: 1-4411-4888-4 (pbk. : alk. paper) 1. Franklin, Aretha. Amazing grace. I. Title. II. Series.
ML420.F778C64 2011
782.421644092–dc23
2011022487

ISBN: PB: 978-1-4411-4888-9

Series: 33 1/3, volume 84

Printed and bound in the United States of America

To find out more about our authors and books visit www.bloomsbury.com and sign up for our newsletters.

Acknowledgments

This book owes its existence to David Barker and everyone at Continuum who know the enduring value of albums, including *Amazing Grace.*

My spiritual big brothers Anthony Heilbut and David Ritz have permanently enriched the studies of gospel and Aretha Franklin.

I've been fortunate to work with an outstanding team at *DownBeat*/Maher Publications, particularly Frank Alkyer, Ed Enright, Jason Koransky, Kevin Maher, Zach Phillips, Bobby Reed, Jennifer Ruban-Gentile, Ara Tirado, and Andy Williams.

It's been edifying, and a great trip, to experience journalism through the daily newspaper trenches at the *Chicago Tribune*, especially because of Lou Carlozo, Greg Kot, Howard Reich, Heidi Stevens, and Kevin M. Williams.

Friends, relatives, and professional associates have helped in numerous ways and I'll always be grateful for: Lisa Bellamore, Peter Berkowitz, Wallace Best, Nathan Brackett, Daphne Brooks, Robert Buerglener, Bill Carpenter, Shalini Chatterjee, Matt Cohen, Steven Dolins, Alan Elliott, James "Al" Finley, Gordon Flagg, Bob Gendron, Jerma Jackson, Virginia Jahnke, Herb Jordan, Robert Kendrick, Nick Macri, Bob Marovich, John Murph, David Nathan, Paul Natkin, James and Susan Neumann, Raúl Niño, Michael Orlove, Jeremy Perney, Amanda Petrusich, James Porter, Michael Randolph, Ben Ratliff, Arno Rotbart, Evan Schofer, Jon Schofer, Scott Sherman, Marc Silver, Ivan Watkins, Stephan Wender, Chris Weston, and Matt Weston.

I thank all those who patiently answered my interview questions, particularly: Inez Andrews, Pastor George Ashford, Archbishop Carl Bean, Marshall Chess, Jessy Dixon, Jimmy Douglass, the late Cornell Dupree, John Ford, Nikki Giovanni, Alexander Hamilton, Barbara Harris, Regina Jones, Joe Mardin, VaShawn Mitchell, Walter Moorehead, Debbie Orange, Gene Paul, Herbert Pickard, Rodena Preston, Bernard "Pretty" Purdie, Chuck Rainey, Eric Reed, Dianne Reeves, Henry Saskowski, and Richard Smallwood.

A student of gospel could not have better teachers,

or better friends, than Chicago's Gay family: Donald, Donna, Bozie, Gregory, Margaret, and the late Geraldine.

I first heard Christian music when my childhood best friend Jeff Harling's choir made me realize that different religions' songs frequently share ideals. My memories of him will always be radiant.

For hospitality on California research trips, all kinds of support and wonderful dinners, I send big hugs to my Los Angeles family: Mel, Sherie, and Helen Scheer.

Even if music journalism has never been a lucrative career, my editor mom and historian dad are the most encouraging parents any writer would ever need.

My wife Lavonne is truly amazing: I owe everything to her diligent research help and unconditional love. This book is dedicated to her.

Chapter One

Aretha Franklin could have proclaimed whatever she wanted when she walked up the aisle of the New Temple Missionary Baptist Church in Watts, Los Angeles, on January 13, 1972. Her performance would be the first of two nights there and her introduction, the audience's cheers, and an arsenal of microphones and cameras, gave her the foundation and anticipation to shout in a voice that had become internationally familiar. Still, at that church, when Franklin wasn't singing, she hardly said anything.

Franklin was away from Detroit, where she was raised, and New York, where she lived, but a longtime friend, Rev. James Cleveland, led the New Temple service in front of his choir and her working band. Another minister, her father, Rev. C. L. Franklin, was in the house — as were her sisters and a couple of mentors. Her *Young, Gifted and Black* album would be released less than two weeks later, but she never mentioned that in the church. Neither did Cleveland nor her father. Aretha's sense of style spoke for itself. On both nights she wore bright gowns, and dangling jeweled earrings, yet not an amount of glitter that could be called distracting. Her eyeliner and lipstick enhanced what may have been a shy smile. During those two nights, she sang religious songs with a fervor that incited ecstatic shouts from the congregation, and almost the same reaction from the seasoned musicians working alongside her. Other than unleashing her luminous vocal sound, nothing that Aretha Franklin said pronounced her as one of the most popular and influential singers on the planet. On those January nights she just seemed appreciative and eager to collaborate. About six months later, Atlantic would release the double-album *Amazing Grace*, which documented those nights. It remains the biggest selling LP of her career.

Franklin never had to say outright how much recording in the church meant to her. But it can be inferred from her 1974 appearance on the television quiz show "What's My Line?" When asked about her trajectory, her answer was the sort of laconic statement that has always typified her interviews: "I did sing in the young people's choir in my father's church — I started there," Franklin said simply. "And from there, here."[1]

She left out a few high points on that quiz show. As the world knows, most of her hit singles had been recorded by that time. National magazines featured her on the cover, and she had become a generational icon even before a nostalgia industry conceived of such a role. Still, Franklin's polite and brief words on "What's My Line?" summing up where she came from, and what she's accomplished, didn't acknowledge any of that, as if none of it mattered. But through her polite terse statement, she indicated the one thing that mattered a great deal.

The familiar Franklin narrative goes like this: Daughter of a famous minister, Aretha Franklin began singing gospel as a girl; crossed over to jazz-inflected pop; achieved little initial success; then, working with a street-smart producer, brought her earliest church background to a grittier take on r&b; became American soul royalty.

All of which contains some truth, yet misses the most interesting part of the story.

Here's another version: Daughter of an influential minister, Aretha Franklin accompanied her father on the gospel circuit, where she remained close

---

[1] Viewed on YouTube.com

with the music's most celebrated singers. She was only about a generation removed from this genre's creation. Going secular, she eventually worked with a consistent team of musicians who ideally complemented her voice during the late '60s and early '70s. Franklin brought that group and her family to that Baptist church in Los Angeles and recorded *Amazing Grace* during those two January nights in 1972. For generations of gospel singers, the album is more influential than any of her internationally adored secular songs. Almost 40 years later, Franklin remained tied to her church roots, holding revivals in Detroit and singing at Albertina Walker's Chicago funeral in 2010, a few weeks before her own serious health concerns curtailed several months of public and media appearances.

So Aretha Franklin began in the church and — as she and her father said time and again — never left. She just stayed on her own terms. Unlike Dinah Washington, she made the road from God to earthly romance a two-way street. Unlike Al Green, she never became ordained while making this circular trip. And, unlike Sam Cooke, few minded when Franklin moved back and forth from this divide. Even today, to call her a gospel artist is not a misnomer. True, her most recognized songs are secular (though maybe not so purely: at the Hollywood Bowl, in June

2009, she ended "Freeway of Love" by calling out to Jesus — an odd juxtaposition, but not that rare).[2] And her mezzo-soprano delivery owes as much — if not more — to her family, friends, and gospel legends such as Clara Ward, as it does to blues/jazz hero Washington. While gospel fans debate whether the music was at its creative height in the late '40s/early–'50s or late-'60s/early-'70s, Franklin grew up in the center of the action during the former era and achieved her artistic and commercial peak throughout the latter.

Amazing Grace also became a milestone because of Franklin's call-and-response with her collaborators. Within the church, singer/pianist/arranger Cleveland's vocal tone and compositions are even more influential than Franklin's voice. He also brought choirs to a higher level of precision. But Cleveland never worked with a more accomplished rhythm section than on this album, primarily Franklin's working band of bassist Chuck Rainey, drummer Bernard "Pretty" Purdie and guitarist Cornell Dupree. The group and environment gave Franklin the space and support to sing with more

---

[2] The combination recurs in r&b performers' arsenal: at the 1989 Chicago Blues Festival, Ernie K. Doe called out to his savior during a 20-minute version of "Mother-in-Law."

freedom than she had when she cranked out two- or three-minute singles throughout the preceding decade.

"It was just an overwhelming sunshine wonderful moment in time," said Atlantic engineer Gene Paul, who worked on *Amazing Grace*. "Because of the love and not worrying about making a hit record. I saw [producer] Jerry Wexler looking at her like she was really in her place. Perhaps the most delightful moment in making a record is not having to be involved in making a hit, and just making beautiful music."

Still, the popular media rarely present her journey from a gospel perspective, and so this album remains frequently overlooked. For instance, when *Rolling Stone* named Franklin the greatest singer of the rock era in November 2008, *Amazing Grace* wasn't mentioned in Mary J. Blige's written tribute that accompanied the cover.[3] A few months after Franklin's 50th birthday in 1992, Rhino released the four-disc compilation, *Queen of Soul: The Atlantic Recordings*, yet included only one song from her most successful LP.

During those two January nights in Los Angeles, Franklin's family, colleagues, and congregants inside

[3] Mary J. Blige, "Aretha Franklin," *Rolling Stone*, November 27, 2008, 73.

the church helped shape the music, but *Amazing Grace* also touched on social and political changes far outside its doors. She took the bold step to co-produce an album that connects the historic music of the African American church, contemporary pop, and Afrocentric fashion, and in so doing presented herself as a modern black woman who could make her own artistic demands. As critics, scholars, and Franklin herself have weighed in on how "Respect" and "Think" reflected the burgeoning black pride movements of the '60s, the optimism that infused *Amazing Grace* conveyed its own meaning during the tumultuous early '70s. Still, while the album looked to the future through its arrangements and delivery, Franklin consciously reached back to the roots of a tradition: most of the songs on the album were those that she heard, and first sang, at her father's side. All of which made this record stand out from the gospel-pop crossovers that had been in vogue at that time. Rather than writing or interpreting new compositions (as The Staple Singers did) or focus on mixing current pop with reworked hymns (as the Edwin Hawkins Singers did), most of the repertoire was written a couple of decades earlier. Few soul stars of that time emphasized an older generation's style and songs on albums. Her contemporaries in rock — The Beatles, Rolling Stones — were not averse to interpreting, say, Little Richard or Howlin' Wolf. But unlike Franklin, they didn't grow up with their earliest influences visiting their homes.

If all of this seems like a heavy load for four sides of vinyl, *Amazing Grace* has shouldered this responsibility for nearly 40 years. Poet Nikki Giovanni, a friend of Franklin, points to the title track for how it bundles the singer's personal history, the state of black America and an image of composer John Newton's immoral career in human trafficking.

"The song itself is, in my opinion, post-civil rights," Giovanni said. "Because you had this slaver who began to understand that, 'Oh, this isn't a good idea selling human beings.' Aretha is just so key to everything: She too is saying, 'We have to change. That's all "Amazing Grace" stands for. It's time to change. We can no longer do what we did. And she's going to be the person to reach generations. She's going to go back to my mother, my grandmother and she's going to go forward. So she's in the same position as what the title of the album is saying. Didn't James Brown sing, 'Money won't change you but time is taking you on/ Get it, get it, get down with it'? But it's not James carrying the cultural weight that Aretha did. I've got nothing against James, but Aretha was a princess, she came with credentials, so she had to be taken seriously."

A note on the source material:

The primary document for this book is the edition of *Amazing Grace* that was released as a double-LP set in 1972. This was the version that its participants are speaking about, and it became certified double platinum 20 years later. But I also use the longer two-CD set that Rhino released as *Amazing Grace: The Complete Recordings* in 1999. This version contains straight recordings of the Thursday, January 13 and Friday, January 14 services. Along with more music, the CD set contains lengthier spoken-word sermons, and differs in running order and mixes. I'll describe the edits as they arise. Information regarding who played on Atlantic sessions, album release dates and chart positions are mostly taken from mid- to late-'90s reissues on Rhino. All quotes are taken from my interviews with the participants, unless otherwise noted.

My descriptions of how the Los Angeles New Temple Missionary Baptist Church looked when Franklin recorded *Amazing Grace* there come from viewing footage of Sydney Pollack's uncompleted film of the recording. I saw the footage in June 2009 and visited the church the next day. During the course of this book's writing, producers Alan Elliott and Herb Jordan along with editor William Steinkamp have been working to complete this project.

Chapter Two

> When pushed, she admits to the continuing gospel influence. "Basically, yes, the feeling is still there and it will always be, more than likely. But if you really wanted to break it down, you could go back even further to more distant roots — if you wanted."
>
> —Valerie Wilmer, "Aretha … Lady Soul," *DownBeat*, August 8, 1968

During Aretha Franklin's first recording session, her strongest feeling may have been fear. It was 1956 and she was ensconced at Detroit's New Bethel Baptist Church, where her father C. L. was a nationwide star of the pulpit. His producer, Joe Von Battle, was on hand to tape the reverend's daughter singing "Precious Lord," and "Never Grow Old." Still, her rough fervor and conviction powered a three-plus octave bulldozer of a voice that squashed trepidations. The songs were in the repertoire of every singer she had admired. Many of those vocalists had spent time in her home, some had become surrogate mothers. At the time those tapes rolled, she was 14 years old.

Aretha Franklin hadn't lived an ordinary Midwestern life when she commanded such haunting religious songs as "There Is a Fountain Filled With Blood." That could be why instead of projecting winsome innocence, she attacked the repertoire as if it could be her last week on Earth. (In contrast, another gospel prodigy around that time — Sylvester Stewart — did sound like a sweet upbeat little kid, although that changed when he became Sly Stone.) But her memoir focuses on the idyllic quotidian parts of her childhood (*Aretha: From These Roots*, written with David Ritz). The Arcadia roller rink was a big deal. Sometime around the age of 10, C. L. Franklin put a box underneath Aretha so she could be near the microphone and she sang in front of 1,500 people at New Bethel.[1] As a teenager, she would've known how her father's orations reached a nationwide audience through his Chess recordings — to this day, Marshall Chess still complains about having to pack Franklin

[1] Bernard Weintraub, "Aretha, So Damn Happy About Her New Album," *The New York Times*, September 28, 2003, A27.

78s in boxes after boxes for radio stations down South. When she started playing the piano at home, the audience would include such family friends as Art Tatum.

Some things were difficult despite, or maybe because of, her father's celebrity. Around the time she made those first recordings, Franklin had given birth to her first child, Clarence. About eight years earlier, her mother, Barbara — a gospel singer — had left the family (for unknown reasons, according to C. L. Franklin's biographer Nick Salvatore) and moved to Buffalo, N.Y. Barbara died there four years later.[2]

Franklin's one comment about this amounted to a few blunt sentences in her memoirs when she mentions hearing her father intone "Your Mother Loves Her Children." But it should be noted that when she went back into the church to record *Amazing Grace*, the timing was close to the twentieth anniversary of her mother's death.

Popular imagery often connects C. L. Franklin's friend Mahalia Jackson to Aretha Franklin in a simplistic Queen of Gospel-to-Queen of Soul lineage, even with their clear vocal and personal differences.

---

[2] Nick Salvatore, *Singing in a Strange Land: C. L. Franklin, the Black Church and the Transformation of America* (New York: Little, Brown, 2005), 122–124.

Jackson did help care for C. L. Franklin's daughters after Barbara's passing. No reason to doubt that, since she was born, Franklin heard Jackson sing "Precious Lord, Take My Hand" many times. Both singers have been known for bold vocal displays that ignore bar lines or usual octave limitations. Symbolism has considerable weight, too; like the parallel of Jackson singing at President John F. Kennedy's inaugural and Franklin performing at the same event 48 years later for President Barack Obama. Nor should Franklin and Jackson's shared association with Dr. Martin Luther King, Jr., be taken lightly. But these cultural affinities don't reflect the sharp vocal and personal contrasts between the two women. Their voices were built differently, and they had distinctive ranges. Jackson was a deep contralto and Franklin is more a mezzo-soprano. Franklin could sculpt her phrasing along with her own piano chords, something that Jackson could not do even with first-rate accompaniment from the devoted Mildred Falls.

Clara Ward and her family group, the Ward Singers, had a more profound impact on Franklin in the '50s and throughout her career. Ward played piano and her chord changes shaped her singing, which brought her closer to Franklin than Jackson. Although an alto, Ward's style resonates through Franklin's take on "How I Got Over," particularly the apparent restraint, expertly timed pauses behind the beat and her leaps in octaves. Franklin also adapted some of Ward's signature stage moves, like dramatically tossing off and throwing down a hat, coat or wig. But the fervor and desperation in the teenage Franklin's voice as she sang those early gospel recordings have no singular precedent.

By no means naive, Franklin undoubtedly has her reasons for claiming to not know about her father's romantic ties to Clara Ward — even as they traveled the world together — although adds in her memoirs that she wouldn't have minded if that connection existed. She seems to be the only person who was not in the know: When Ward's sister Willa Ward-Royster was approached to speak for this book, she politely declined, saying, "I didn't know Aretha Franklin that well — it was Clara and her father who were sweethearts."

Franklin also encountered another key influence — The Caravans — on the gospel touring circuit of the '50s. The Caravans became a launching pad for talented members who would go on to lead their own groups, and Albertina Walker kept the institution going until her death in October 2010. One of their standout numbers was "Mary, Don't You Weep," which featured singer Inez Andrews' bluesy vamp and original sermonette about Lazarus rising from the tomb. Although the gospel genre has always been filled with as much rivalry and bitterness as its secular counterparts, Andrews never felt any envy toward the upstart with a famous preacher dad.

"We used to call her The Baby Singer because she was one of the baddest baby singers you've ever seen," Andrews said. "The baby would outsing the young, the middle aged, the old, the crippled, the blind. She could outsing all of us. She'd outsing even the ones she was packaged with — the Clara Ward Singers. She was just dynamite. When Aretha sang, everybody would stop singing and go to listening, that's how good she was. And still is."

James Cleveland served as The Caravans' musical director and accompanist. He was 11 years older than Franklin and he also linked her directly to gospel's pioneers. Their backgrounds and connections to that generation were considerably different. While Franklin was the daughter of a popular minister in Detroit, Cleveland grew up poor in Chicago's South Side. In 1968, he told *Ebony* that he was Mahalia Jackson's paperboy and would put an ear to a door to hear her singing while she worked as a hairdresser.[3] Jackson helped cook Franklin's family dinners. Franklin had a piano at home while Cleveland told

[3] "James Cleveland: King of Gospel," *Ebony*, November 1968, 74.

Anthony Heilbut he had to practice on keys that he drew on his family's windowsill.[4]

As if Cleveland always knew that music was his means to escape from poverty, he emphasized volume, especially as a boy soprano at the hugely influential Thomas A. Dorsey's Pilgrim Baptist Church. He permanently strained his voice when he strove to stand out from the rest of the choir. Dorsey noticed him.

Dorsey's compositions, especially "Precious Lord, Take My Hand" in 1932, transformed black church music from reliance on older hymns and spirituals to the twentieth century blues-derived genre known as gospel. His accomplishments didn't end with pen and paper. He also had a role in creating the gospel group concept, and hiring Roberta Martin as his pianist. Martin would form the Roberta Martin Singers, which featured Cleveland's compositions. Cleveland wanted to sound like one of his heroes — baritone Eugene Smith of the Martin Singers — but his own voice was not as fluid. Cleveland claimed similarities to Louis Armstrong, and some shared inflections were there, if not the range. His raspy speaking voice kind of resembled another Chicagoan who

[4]Anthony Heilbut, *The Gospel Sound* (New York: Limelight Edition, 1997), 207.

came along much later: comedian Bernie Mac. Still, Cleveland could jump into energetic falsetto yelps that would rock churches and his writing, arranging and band-leading skills as a prodigy compensated for any lack of vocal range or technique. As Franklin mentions in her memoirs, he had already written the Martin Singers' "Grace is Sufficient" by the time he was 16 and she remembers that, "his piano technique was pure gospel, with big chords that were exciting and rich. James heard harmonies in his head that most people missed."[5]

Cleveland lived with the Franklin family for a while, but, according to Aretha, got booted at some point in the early '50s when he took some banana pudding that C. L. was saving for himself. Franklin also recalled to Phyl Garland in a 1967 *Ebony* interview that, "There's a whole lot of earthiness in the way he sings, and what he was feelin,' I was feelin', but I just didn't know how to put it across. The more I watched him, the more I got out of it."[6]

In Matt Dobkin's book about Franklin's Atlantic debut, *I Never Loved a Man the Way I Loved You*, he reiterates that Cleveland shaped her facility on the

---

[5] Aretha Franklin and David Ritz, *Aretha: From These Roots* (New York: Villard, 1999), 41.
[6] Phyl Garland, "Aretha Franklin — 'Sister Soul'," *Ebony*, October 1967, 48.

piano, and that this instrumental skill helped her stand out from every other pop vocalist of the '60s.[7] But others insist that, even as a teenager, she had already stepped away from his influence.

Musician/educator Adrian York mentions of her playing, "at the end of every line, she puts in a right-hand fill, often ascending spread inversions of the chord or major pentatonic octave lines."[8] These inversions would indicate that she had picked up on the flourishes from legends such as Art Tatum when they visited her family's living room. A keyboardist who always remained in C. L. Franklin's good graces, Herbert Pickard, has his own observations. He was the minister's favorite pianist and accompanied him on revivals. Pickard also played organ for the Gospel Harmonettes, which featured singer/political activist Dorothy Love Coates. Still living in Detroit, and now in his upper 70s, he saw the early dynamic among C. L. and Aretha Franklin, as well as Cleveland. Pickard, a fan of Erroll Garner, also showed Cleveland how several minor chords could be used in gospel, yet he had differences with his

---

[7] Matt Dobkin, *I Never Loved a Man the Way I Love You* (New York: St. Martin's Griffin, 2004), 74–75.

[8] Adrian York, "Keyboard Techniques," *The Cambridge Companion to Blues and Gospel Music* (Cambridge: Cambridge University Press, 2002), 139.

friend's approach, which he contrasts to a teenage Aretha.

"James was hard on that instrument," Pickard said. "He played heavy. I probably wouldn't have told him that. I don't think he needed me to tell him that he was banging on the piano — I seen him press the pedals so hard, they'd break underneath the keyboard. Very hard on the instrument, but he was James. Aretha had the heavy hand, but was not as hard as James. Aretha's playing was nice, it was decent."

In other words, even just sitting down at the piano, Cleveland demanded to be heard. Since gospel performer/scholar Horace C. Boyer observed that one of the characteristics of typical gospel instrumental accompaniment is "hardly any pedaling for piano,"[9] Cleveland stood out without even opening his mouth.

Cleveland's role in Franklin's development wasn't limited to piano technique, and this would be spelled out years later, in his spoken remarks heard on the *Complete Sessions* version of *Amazing Grace*. Early on the first night of recording, he mentions that there are hymns everyone in the Baptist church knows, and then he, Aretha Franklin, the choir and band launch

[9] Horace C. Boyer, "Gospel Music Comes of Age," *Black World*, November 1973, 48.

into the traditional, "What a Friend we Have in Jesus." Shortly later, before "How I Got Over," he declares that they'd play a Sanctified rhythm, representing a different denomination. The tempo picks up and the church sounds like it is about to launch. Franklin's own response was more subdued. Pollack's film of *Amazing Grace* shows that when Cleveland asks if anyone in the house "knows anything about the Sanctified church," she simply, knowingly, raises her hand.

With just these words and this brief musical intro, Cleveland brings in the "more distant roots" that Franklin told Valerie Wilmer about in this chapter's epigraph. While Cleveland grew up in Chicago's Baptist churches, and became a minister in the denomination, he also built a following within the Church of God in Christ (COGIC). COGIC is the largest Pentecostal denomination and many Pentecostal churches are referred to as Sanctified. The gospel tradition that Franklin and Cleveland drew upon has its roots in the early twentieth century with the emergence of Sanctified churches. African American Baptist and Sanctified churches shared a history, traditions and occasional concert billings, but there were key divergences. A bit of background:

In simple terms, Baptists believe in salvation through immersion (that overly familiar image of the robes, the river) and the Pentecostal churches believe that the Holy Spirit becomes manifest through such phenomena as glossolalia (speaking in tongues). But the historical differences and cultural contexts of the denominations, particularly in black America, go deeper.

Black Baptist congregations spun away from their white counterparts as African Americans sought religious autonomy in the latter eighteenth century, according to historians C. Eric Lincoln and Lawrence H. Mamiya in their book, *The Black Church in the African American Experience*. The number of black Baptists, and their striving for self-determination, increased in reaction to America through the legacy of slavery, Civil War, Reconstruction and segregation. They were also solidly organized and through the National Baptist Convention of America worked against racial violence and discrimination. The Convention also published the song collection *Gospel Pearls* in 1921, which codified and spread the music throughout black churches across the United States. The hymnal included notation and lyrics for what would become standard versions of "Amazing Grace," "God Will Take Care of You," and "What a Friend." In the '60s, a schism divided the ranks over C. L. Franklin's ally Dr. Martin Luther King, Jr.'s plan for civil disobedience to protest segregation. Franklin's family remained loyal to their friend.

Unlike the Baptists, the Pentecostal church is a black American ecclesiastical tradition that did not form through breaking away from an older, white denomination, yet grew out of the indigenous Holiness movement. Pentecostalism got off the ground at 312 Azusa Street in Los Angeles in 1906 when William Seymour, a minister and son of former slaves, came to town with accounts of miracle faith healing and the imminent visit of the Holy Ghost. He formed his own church when more established black Holiness congregations found his depictions of spiritual visitations and spiritual manifestations, such as speaking in tongues, too radical. His Pentecostalism also attracted white followers, but this integration didn't last more than 18 years.[10] COGIC was founded in Memphis in the early twentieth century (the city was also Aretha Franklin's birthplace).

Historically, social status has divided Baptists and Pentecostals. For a long time, being Sanctified signified being from a poorer, or more disenfranchised, class. This situation would have been true when Franklin was growing up, although, as Lincoln and Mamiya stated, by the '80s, those strata were breaking down. Members of both denominations

[10] R. J. Smith, *The Great Black Way* (New York: Public Affairs, 2006), 158–172.

have always lived near each other. Within their Detroit neighborhood, C. L. and Aretha Franklin were able to absorb the doctrines, sermons, deliveries, and rhythms of any number of faiths. So those storefront churches would have been unavoidable to a young Aretha Franklin. On the East Coast, Jacqui Verdell, a soaring mezzo-soprano who inspired a young Aretha Franklin, grew up COGIC. Heilbut describes their community bonds and theological directions throughout his chapters, "The Holiness Church" and "The Traveling Saints," in *The Gospel Sound* ("Saints" is the term used to describe Pentecostal adherents — which shows their strict piety). He describes "the archetypal Holiness song" as a "slow chant usually sung as the service begins, or when the spirit has erupted in an outburst of frenetic shouts."

"To go to a Holiness church when the spirit's high, and the world's impurities are cast out into the streets from whence they came, to hear the saints assenting, is to believe that music can transport one to 'higher ground'," Heilbut adds.[11]

Even though the Pentecostal Church originated in Los Angeles, black congregants in that city didn't embrace gospel music during the '30s and

---

[11] Heilbut, 177.

'40s, according to musicologist Jacqueline Cogdell DjeDje.[12] Hymns, spirituals, and congregational singing were preferred over gospel and its proto-rock 'n' roll rhythms.

By the early '50s, Sanctified groups in the mid-West, like Chicago's Gay Sisters, were churning out gospel hits; their startling harmonies transformed the hymn "God Will Take Care of You" into a 1952 mega-seller on Savoy. Equally important, while the Sanctified and Holiness Churches were still scorned as low-class among larger, more mainstream churches at that time, the Gay Sisters — like the Ward Singers — carried themselves with the sort of sartorial elegance that would have attracted a young Aretha Franklin. Cleveland was also close to the Gay family, so much so that the youngest Gay Sister, the late pianist Geraldine Gay, mentioned that, as a teenager, he was her first boyfriend.

"When I asked him what he loved the most about me," Geraldine Gay said, "he'd always say my hair and clothes."

Further away from Franklin and Cleveland's Detroit–Chicago sphere, young musicians, who would

[12] Jacqueline Cogdell DjeDje, "Gospel Music in the Los Angeles Black Community: A Historical Overview," *Black Music Research Journal*, Vol. 9, no. 1 (Spring, 1989), 43–45.

become her key collaborators, immersed themselves in the different churches' gospel lineages. Years before drummer Bernard Purdie became Franklin's musical director, he grew up in the small town of Elkton, Maryland, where his parents were devout Methodists (he adopted the nickname "Pretty" when nearby kids kept mispronouncing his name). He said that he used to play at "what we used to call the holy-rolly church because they had music and they were slammin' — they were really slammin'." (Purdie's term for what's commonly called the "holy roller" church is one of his unique phrases.) As a young drummer, he kept on making the rounds and when he wanted to play he noticed that those Sanctified churches had their own requirements:

> What made it different is when you get the spirit in the Baptist church, you had a one that you had to deal with. "Dealing with the one, and also dealing with the three-quarter time was the heaviest part of the Baptist. In the holy-rolly church, it was the backbeat, dealing with straight time, quarters, quarters, quarters. And when you doubled the tempo, you had to come off of the drum, off the music so light, so fast that nothing stayed on the ground. It was moving because the people danced that, that's how they moved their bodies. They moved and then they would go, like insane. People had eyes rolling back because they

were shouting. So you had to stay with the Sanctified sound. [voices] Chap, chap, chap, chap. You had to do that and you couldn't think in terms of mm-mm chap, mm-mm-chap. That came from country music and blues, and that's what we did all those years with the gospel thing. That's what the holy-rolly church did. Baptist was more sophisticated. They did the triplets. Mm — chang-chang. That's how they got into it, they clapped and stomped and you had to play the music that way. And when you had something that was a ballad that was slow, it was also in 3/4 time or 12/4. If you didn't have the 3/4 you had the 12/4, which now represents 12/8 most of the time. But the 12/4 was heavy in the '40s and '50s. You had the tambourine that went off that, it was really, truly awesome.

Not all of the church-raised musicians who worked in Franklin's circle during the late '60s and early '70s felt this way. Bassist Chuck Rainey, who grew up Pentecostal in Cleveland and Youngstown, Ohio, has a different perspective:

The feel of the music is hard to explain. If you're not from it, it's hard to get to it, or if you haven't had the experience of being around it for a length of time. Ray Charles demonstrates that when he plays 'My Country 'Tis of Thee' in a 12/8 feel. Of course, it's 4/4, but really a 12/8, very slow with a lot of feeling. When it gets very rhythmic, it's just a feel that's been very important to me. There is no difference in

> Baptist or Pentecostal. Just plain Christian Church. Music was all the same. Only thing different is the doctrine.

One of those doctrinal differences 50 years ago meant that, as a member of a large Baptist church, Franklin had an easier time crossing over into secular music and back than if she were from a more insular Sanctified congregation. She had a different path than her friend (and teenage crush) Sam Cooke — the son of Holiness Reverend Samuel Cook in Chicago — who caused many of the faithful to gnash their teeth when he left gospel stardom to record "Lovable" and "You Send Me" (although Rev. Cook didn't mind the money that resulted). Some devout Baptists were upset at Franklin's worldly involvement, but her early church audience never abandoned her. It helped that Rev. C. L. Franklin was such a commanding presence.

"I always liked blues," C. L. Franklin said to scholar Jeff Todd Titon. "There were some people, some church people who didn't approve it, blues, but they didn't understand that it was part of their cultural heritage."[13]

---

[13] Reverend C. L. Franklin, *Give Me This Mountain* Urbana, IL.: University of Illinois, 1989), 5.

So it didn't take much soul searching for the Reverend Franklin to embrace his daughter's decision to follow Cooke's secular path in 1960 when, at 18, she began recording such tracks as "Today I Sing the Blues." Salvatore relates a dramatic moment in the spring of that year when the two performed at the Handy Festival of Music in Memphis, Tennessee. C. L. Franklin just said that whoever didn't like his daughter's musical choices could leave.[14] Few did.

Aretha Franklin articulated her reasons for moving into secular music as a guest columnist for the black newspaper *New York Amsterdam News* on August 26, 1961, around a year after she began singing in nightclubs. She cites Cooke, Sister Rosetta Tharpe, and especially Mahalia Jackson for their integrity while performing in popular arenas. But the 19-year-old singer also perceptively connects religion, the blues, and the civil rights movement.

"I don't think that in any manner I did the Lord a disservice when I made up my mind two years ago to switch over," Franklin wrote. "After all, the blues is a music born out of the slavery day sufferings of my people. Every song in the blues vein has a story to tell of love, frustrations and heartaches. I think that

[14] Salvatore, 239.

because true democracy hasn't overtaken us here that we as a people find the original blues songs still have meaning for us."[15]

[15] Aretha Franklin, "From Gospel to Jazz is Not Disrespect for The Lord!," *New York Amsterdam News*, August 26, 1961, 17.

Chapter Three

Aretha Franklin's six years at Columbia (1960–1965) have usually been depicted as producer John Hammond's occasionally successful — but ultimately misguided — effort to turn her into a jazz-pop-r&b-Broadway singer. Then, the story goes, when she signed to Atlantic in 1966, Jerry Wexler had the sense to sit her at the piano, let her gospel rhythms and raw delivery flow, and her hits poured out of a newfound roots-conscious sensibility. Franklin's childhood friend, poet/author Al Young, claims that, at Columbia, "She could perform cabaret songs persuasively — even beautifully — but her heart was never really in it."[1] Young does not reveal how he knew her intentions. Peter Guralnick writes in *Sweet*

[1] Al Young, "Aretha Franklin," salon.com, August 3, 1999.

Soul Music that, "she had achieved a considerable underground reputation, but when she signed with Atlantic in November 1966, she was without any real sense of artistic or commercial direction. It had been five years since she last had an r&b hit, her latest offerings on Columbia were a peculiar mix of show tunes and schmaltz."[2]

But Franklin's Columbia years were more crucial than wasted detours on her path to soul superstardom. They also contributed directly to her artistic peak on *Amazing Grace*, perhaps more than her widely popular initial Atlantic albums. Perceptions of this period should change with the 2011 release of the 11-CD/1-DVD box set, *Take a Look: Aretha Franklin Complete on Columbia* (Sony/Legacy).

She couldn't have found a producer whose track record in gospel, blues and jazz went as far back as Hammond. He presented Rosetta Tharpe and the Golden Gate Quartet at the From Spirituals to Swing concerts at Carnegie Hall in 1938 and 1939 and signed Mahalia Jackson. That was along with his noted professional involvement with Bessie Smith, Count Basie, Billie Holiday, and numerous other secular and religious musical giants. Around

[2] Peter Guralnick, *Sweet Soul Music* (New York: Harper and Row, 1986), 332.

the time that she signed to Columbia, Hammond produced the live recording, The Abyssinian Baptist Gospel Choir's *Shakin' the Rafters*, which Professor Alex Bradford directed. Bradford — a formidable singer, pianist, and composer — was another hero to James Cleveland. This live album of a high-powered small instrumental group meeting a large choir was one forerunner to *Amazing Grace*. One reason was because the Abyssinian Baptist album featured an unusual (for the time) focus on those core instrumentalists, particularly pianist Willie James McPhatter.

"It would be a good thing for some Negro organizations to remember the next time they choose someone to honor for his contribution to humanity not forget the name of John Hammond," Franklin wrote in the *New York Amsterdam News* (1961). In a later sign of continued mutual affinity, Hammond would write liner notes for *Amazing Grace*, even though it was on a competitor's label.

Columbia also provided Franklin a platform to pay tribute to, and break away from, her early influences, such as Dinah Washington.[3] At a remarkably young age, she delivered sophisticated American songbook

[3] Michael Awkward contends that Franklin's 1964 Washington tribute album, *Unforgettable*, was essential for her to establish a unique identity in his book, *Soul Covers* (Durham, N.C.: Duke University Press, 2007).

standards — with more earthiness than her contemporary supper club acts — yet could also ease into romantic pop with more strength than her teenage competitors. That "Skylark" and "One Step Ahead" didn't become massive hits were neither the fault of the singer nor her producers. Heilbut points out that Franklin's version of the American pop standard, "That Lucky Old Sun" on *The Electrifying Aretha Franklin* (1962) album, was most likely the model for singer Cassietta George's delivery on The Caravans' "Walk Around Heaven All Day" two years later — Franklin's bluesy nuance, inspired one-word repetitions and behind-the-beat timing in particular. Franklin also slowly emphasized the sense of impoverished tragedy in the lyrics that, say, Frankie Laine's hit version, didn't. In other words, a woman who just turned 20 and had supposedly left the church was already influencing one of the gospel groups that had inspired her. Not so coincidentally, her friend Cleveland co-wrote The Caravans' hit.[4] Cleveland also stepped away from composing religious songs to write one of Franklin's early pure romantic pop tunes, "Nobody Like You," on *The Electrifying Aretha Franklin*.

[4]"Walk Around Heaven All Day" is available on *Vee-Jay: The Definitive Collection* (Shout! Factory), a four-disc box that compiles songs from Chicago's pre-eminent late '50s/early '60s r&b and gospel label.

Franklin's time at Columbia often compelled her to work with a proficient small band. Her debut LP, *Aretha*, included a veteran jazz rhythm section of pianist Ray Bryant (who grew up playing gospel), bassist Bill Lee, and drummer James "Osie" Johnson. During these years, she quickly developed improvisational skills — an ability to add in subtle inflections that put her on the same wavelength as these urbane and experienced musicians. This combination of backgrounds would have been closer to her later Atlantic years — leading Rainey, Purdie, and Dupree — on *Young, Gifted and Black* and *Amazing Grace* than the Southern r&b players she used on her 1966 and 1967 Atlantic sessions at studios such as Muscle Shoals in Alabama.

Also in the early '60s, Mahalia Jackson performed with a first-rate jazz rhythm section of drummer Shelly Manne, guitarist Barney Kessel, and bassist Red Mitchell on late-night NBC television spots.[5] Franklin would perform in a similar format, and with an orchestra, on "The Steve Allen Show" in 1964. Even if Franklin and Jackson's affiliations with Columbia were not directly connected to Jackson's televised shows, the younger singer must have

[5] Mahalia Jackson, *A Gospel Calling: Mahalia Jackson Sings* [DVD] (Image Entertainment, 2010).

seen them and possibly became aware of how this combination of gospel vocal performance and jazz instrumentation could reach something approaching a mass audience.

Chapter Four

> I suppose the [Black] Revolution influenced me a great deal, but I must say that mine was a very personal evolution — an evolution of the me in myself. But then I suppose that the whole meaning of the Revolution is very much tied up with that sort of thing, so it certainly must have helped what I was trying to do for myself.
>
> —Aretha Franklin to Charles L. Sanders in "Aretha: A Close-up Look at Sister Superstar," *Ebony*, December 1971

At the time Aretha Franklin spoke with Charles L. Sanders for *Ebony* in her Manhattan apartment, she had already recorded the hits that would keep her in designer gowns and extravagant hats for life. The interview would have been around the summer of 1971; there's a reference to her upcoming album *Young, Gifted and Black*, which she had finished recording in February of that year. Franklin briefly mentioned her plans for *Amazing Grace*, saying that she was "real excited" about the gospel recording and that "it's going to be done with James Cleveland and we'll record it in a church with a real good choir." Franklin also seems to be thinking about the era's social movements. The article begins with Sanders noticing that the singer's bookshelf includes *The Negro Handbook*, Frantz Fanon's *A Dying Colonialism* and "that far out *Eros and Civilization* by Angela Davis' old professor, Dr. Herbert Marcuse." As usual, Franklin said little, but the article does point to how she had reinvented herself since 1966.

When Dobkin wrote about Franklin's move to Atlantic from Columbia in *I Never Loved a Man the Way I Loved You*, he attests that, despite portrayals to the contrary, Wexler did not just take her back to church when she signed to his company. He adds what made her early Atlantic records command the wide audience that alluded her earlier: "The novelty of Aretha's first Atlantic releases, the element that pushed her into the popular-music stratosphere was not gospel fervor (though that certainly helped). It was sex."[1] Possibly, but that's not quite the whole story, and one could also counter that a reason why

[1] Dobkin, 13.

Franklin's church followers did not abandon her was that she didn't ooze sexuality to the extent of, say, Marvin Gaye. And she usually didn't mix up two different concepts of love as strangely as her male Detroit counterpart did when he trailed off "Let's Get It On" with his own context for the word "Sanctified." She chose a different role.

After all, it wasn't just sensuality that put Franklin's version of Otis Redding's "Respect" in *Jet*'s Soul Brothers Top 20 poll, and awarded her a citation from Dr. Marin Luther King, Jr.'s Southern Christian Leadership convention in the summer of 1967.[2] Whether Franklin asked for it or not, she became a cultural heroine in a way that set her apart from such aggressively sexual predecessors as Dinah Washington. By 1971, the empowerment that "Respect" and "Think" embodied turned even more overt in her blazing rendition of Nina Simone's "Young, Gifted and Black." She also started to front a working band that sounded at home backing her in New York and Miami studios, the epicenter of San Francisco's rock scene, and, ultimately, the church where she, and most of that group, began. It's the sort of skilled and sympathetic unit that would be the vehicle for any musical advances. Her songs became

[2] Garland, 47.

longer, and stretched out over new, different and often free-flowing rhythms: she achieved the sense of liberation that her voice always demanded. That Franklin was also delving deeper, and more openly, into gospel fervor at that time wasn't paradoxical.

Much of what's been written about Franklin during this period points toward a newfound sense of confidence, albeit one mixed with an aura of mystery that lasts to this day.[3] As the '60s concluded, she ended her marriage and professional connection to Ted White. For whatever reason, Franklin avoided the recording studios for several months at a time between 1968–1970, much to Wexler's chagrin. When she did show up, the results were hits that defined the times ("Think," "I Say a Little Prayer" from *Aretha Now* in mid-1968) or are reminders that she still could have been a prominent jazz vocalist (the mis-titled *Soul '69*). She also delved into the Sanctified rhythms and call-and-response vocals on her composition "Spirit in the Dark," the title track of her summer 1970 album. The lyrics picked up from Wilson Pickett's exhortations to dance and some nursery rhymes, but the title itself comes straight from Sanctified churches' belief in feeling the holy spirit — and one

[3] Among many examples is Wexler's memoir (written with Ritz), *Rhythm and the Blues* (New York: Knopf, 1993).

could speculate if the "dark" suggests a negative (troubled times) or positive (pigmentation).[4] With piano lines and crescendos sounding as strong as her voice, the beat is the most direct line to a storefront church that she had recorded for Atlantic up to that point. Despite such exuberance, her muted comments about it are oblique.

"Well, it's true that I have to really feel a song before I'll deal with it, and just about every song I do is based on an experience I've had or an experience that someone I know has gone through," Franklin told Sanders in *Ebony*. "'Spirit in the Dark'? Hmmmh ... that's one I'd rather not talk about. It's very, very personal and I don't want to get into it right now."

It also wasn't the only gospel-shaped song that she recorded back then. Rainey played bass on her 1971 single, "Spanish Harlem," and refers its "cross between an eighth-note feel and a shuffle."

"That's the gospel, Pentecostal feel where you're really trying to nail what the groove is," Rainey added. "If you want to write it down for somebody, you can't. You just have to sort of listen to it and feel it. But in playing with her, she brought out another

---

[4]The "ride, Sally ride" line derives from Pickett's hit, "Mustang Sally," which Sir Mack Rice wrote with an assist from Franklin.

energy. It's a kind of feel that's not descriptive. I always try, but it's very difficult."

Her performances were also infrequent, although when she appeared onstage in the spring of 1970, Franklin expressed ambitious plans, especially an ongoing involvement with traditional church music. Her intentions included bringing gospel to Broadway with her sister Carolyn, and a television special in Israel to be called "Aretha in the Holy Land."[5] When Franklin performed at the Las Vegas International Hotel on June 8, 1970 (her first concert in almost a year), she included Albertina Walker and The Caravans on the bill and would continue touring with this group into the following year. She also insisted on the hotel hiring an all-black ensemble for the show, which must have been an audacious request for this historically segregated city.[6]

Franklin's refocus on gospel intertwined with early 1970's cultural discourse. For someone growing up in C. L. Franklin's family, the black consciousness movement of that era was not a jolt. Much of the organizational force behind the civil rights movement was built, and debated, within black churches, and

---

[5] Ed Ochs, "Soul Sauce," *Billboard*, May 23, 1970, 50, and Edward M. Smith, "Gospel Scene," *Billboard*, June 6, 1970, 40.
[6] Laura Deni, "Las Vegas," *Billboard*, June 27, 1970, 55.

the institutions' music and musicians have always been there. In particular, when Aretha Franklin was a child, she would've seen her father chastise the National Association for the Advancement of Colored People (NAACP) for not doing enough to organize Detroit's African American communities, and witnessed his equally daring support of the young Dr. Martin Luther King, Jr. She and Mahalia Jackson remained alongside King, and Franklin sang "Precious Lord, Take My Hand" at his funeral.

In the post-King era, Franklin's cultural embrace became more public and took on an artistic dimension. In her memoirs, she states that much of this came from her new boyfriend, Ken Cunningham. He's described in terms of the Black Arts Movement, which was burgeoning not far from their New York home, and included Nikki Giovanni. Franklin mentions Cunningham's plans for a black-owned fashion business, the New Breeders, which would feature African-inspired clothes. When I asked Giovanni how much Franklin's thinking at this time reflected the Black Aesthetic concept — as articulated by herself and such other writers as Larry Neal — she simply replied, "Aretha was the black aesthetic."

"Daddy had been preaching black pride for decades, and we as a people had rediscovered how beautiful black truly was and were echoing, 'Say it loud, I'm black and I'm proud.'" Franklin told Ritz. "Wolf [Ken Cunningham] and I embodied that pride. I stopped shaving my eyebrows and using pencils and went back to a natural look with a much lighter touch. I lost weight and wore my hair in an Afro; I began to appreciate myself as a beautiful black woman."[7]

Just as explicitly, she recorded Simone's "Young, Gifted and Black" in August 1970. The song's message, written by a Methodist minister's granddaughter who Franklin admired, speaks for itself. Franklin also leads a pulpit-influenced call-and-response with her gospel-rooted back-up singers, The Sweet Inspirations. The changes in her group at that time proved equally crucial. Rainey and guitarist Cornell Dupree played on this song, and Purdie worked on half the other tracks of Franklin's album of the same name. While Franklin had top sidemen throughout her earlier Atlantic sessions, this new core rhythm section essentially became a working band. All three had played alongside the dynamic Texas-bred, New York-based saxophonist King Curtis in the mid '60s. Curtis, a favorite of Franklin and Wexler, didn't so much straddle the borders among r&b, rock, and hard bop, but annihilated the gates. They also shared early experiences in the black church, albeit Purdie and

[7] Franklin and Ritz, 128–129.

Rainey more than Dupree. The other keyboardists on the *Young, Gifted and Black* album — Cleveland's protégé Billy Preston and Donny Hathaway — had also been immersed in similar religious backgrounds. If the principles of pride, strength, and mutual respect were hallmarks of the Black Arts Movement and African American spirituality, this group lived it, according to Purdie:

> We listened to one another and out of respect for what we were doing, we felt that nobody could come between us and move us out of our space. To allow yourself to do your thing, you have to have other people supporting you and we supported each other so well, so much with the rhythm, we were never thinking about solo work. Just rhythm. You just wanted to have the biggest and tightest rhythm section in the world and nobody could come in and squeeze you out. That sound incorporated itself with everybody around us, and then they could just sweeten the pot when they wanted to add a piano, another guitar or something. But the rhythm section was always super, super tight because of the respect we had for each other. It wasn't about us, it wasn't about solo work, it was about a section.

The affinity has lasted.

"If I were a drummer, I'd play exactly like Bernard and if I were a guitar player, I'd hope to play rhythm like Cornell," Rainey said.

This shared respect came about even with their considerably different personalities. Dupree grew up in Curtis' hometown of Fort Worth and played r&b in Texas bars until the saxophonist brought him to New York to work alongside him in his own band and in a host of the city's top recording sessions (along with Rainey, they toured the U.S.A. with The Beatles in 1965). Dupree impressed Purdie because, as he says, "his solos were always the blues." And Dupree impressed just about everyone for his uncanny ability to play lead and rhythm guitar interchangeably, or simultaneously. While he allowed himself to say, with a laugh, "I was dangerous in the studios, I was just rampaging with sessions," his description of his technique revealed his humility. As Dupree said:

> It's something you develop when you back yourself up, when you don't have anybody to back you up. You got to just make it happen to make it a full band. To sound as big as you can, to do as much as you can to make it good. When you're playing, you want something to back you up: You play your lead part and if you see an empty spot, you jump in there to fill it up. Someone else is playing, you want to jump in and back them up to make them sound good. And that's the way I look at it — fill it up and make it sound good for the other person.

Rainey backed-up soul groups and checked out jazz bassists in New York. He adds that the city's diverse environment made his colleagues more aggressive and versatile than the Southern-based musicians who backed Franklin's earlier Atlantic recordings. Wexler has said he admired Rainey's playing technique called "sliding tenths."[8] The bassist said that this way of reaching low notes and high octave notes at the same time (on open E, A, D, and G strings) came from watching older upright players in those Manhattan jazz clubs, especially Milt Hinton, Earl May, and Richard Davis. And from the way he was built for his instrument.

"Coming from guitar to the bass, my hands are kind of thick and big and there were a lot of things I wanted to do on the guitar that I just couldn't because the guitar was just not my instrument," Rainey said. "The strings are too small and too close, and so the bass is perfect."

Purdie has generally been depicted as the effervescent egotist of the group: the soul-jazz equivalent of a young Muhammad Ali. *The New York Times* reported that, "For years he showed up at sessions with two professionally made signs, which he would

---

[8] Josh Alan Friedman, *Tell the Truth Until They Bleed* (San Francisco: Backbeat Books, 2008), 189.

place on music stands near his kit. 'You done hired the hit maker,' read one. 'If you need me, call me, the little old hit maker,' said the other."[9] That image almost contrasts with what he told *DownBeat* in 1971: "'I've given up trying to be the best — nobody can do it. There is always someone better. Now all I want to be is the prettiest.'"[10]

In either case, the gregarious drummer's reputation stems from his pattern that has been called the Purdie Shuffle. It's a fast, tightly syncopated, fluid groove that he created through unexpected hits on the high-hat, bass, and snare, and modeled on the sounds of trains roaring past his Maryland childhood home:

> We had a train station in Elkton and the train could take off, or slow down, at speeds unheard of. It was a sound that I tried to recreate by trying to make that sound go forward. Energy. And it is all about energy, it is all about making a feel and putting yourself in the body of this locomotion. That's the way I looked at music. I always looked at it as a forward motion and keeping everybody happy.

---

[9] David Segal, "A Signature Shuffle Enjoys a New Life," *The New York Times*, March 31, 2009, C1.
[10] Gene Gray, "Bernard Purdie: Soul Beat Mavin," *DownBeat*, January 21, 1971, 18.

The drummer's early experiences in the churches also informed the Purdie Shuffle. But he adds that the pacing of the music in a church service was not always compatible with the tempos he added to his percussive movements. Purdie summarized his technique as: "You have to give it a chance to sink in, that means watching people's body movements, how they moved their feet, how they dance, how they sway."

All of it came together in the first song that this group recorded with Franklin, her luminous "Rock Steady," which was taped at Miami's Criteria Studios on February 16, 1971, and which appeared on *Young, Gifted and Black*. It's a deep funk track, with Purdie's beat driving the initial propulsion. Guest percussionist Dr. John joins in and underpins Franklin's assertive and warm voice woven along with Hathaway's organ lines. Just as Franklin and her sisters Erma and Carolyn had added hip urban slang in the call-and-response section of her version of "Respect" ("sock it to me") four years earlier, she did the same for this hit single ("what it is"). The song also sounds like it was looking ahead to the next decade's r&b. The group's method showed why they'd be able to successfully record naturally live in a church the following year. As Rainey said:

> Bernard and I had worked so many sessions in New York together, we were sort of like twins. Actually, our birthdays are six days apart. We're in Miami and where they had the band staying was different from where Jerry Wexler, [producer] Tommy Dowd and [engineer] Gene Paul were staying. Usually when we started those sessions, they had one car pick up the band, and another pick up those people. This particular day they were about an hour late. Because we all knew each other and were a family, Aretha would just sit down, she would show all the songs that she wrote. We wanted to do 'Rock Steady,' we sat down, and she decided to put it down for reference. So we just laid down the track. When [arranger] Arif [Mardin] and those people came to the studio, we began to work on the song. They tried all morning to try and work on the song, but never got to the feel of what we already laid down. It's a run down before everybody got there. When you're free like that, you're having fun.

Franklin must have also noticed how her friend and early mentor Cleveland was flourishing in California. His rise from wrenching poverty on Chicago's South Side to success as a gospel innovator in Los Angeles is reason enough for his own biography. A laudatory feature in the November 1968 issue of *Ebony* begins with Cleveland at the Apollo telling the audience how he was once so poor he had "no food on my table … no shoes on my feet …" and from there to his ten-room

Spanish style house in Los Angeles' Leimert Park neighborhood. That scene conjures images from the video to Biggie Smalls' "Juicy" decades later but without the rapper's heterosexual machismo. Along with the 275 songs Cleveland wrote, it's mentioned that he taught Franklin "much of what she knows about piano."[11]

Cleveland also may have shown her more than a few things about songwriting, particularly in the building of tempo and tension to the ecstatic levels of "Jesus Saves" from his album *James Cleveland and the Angelic Choir, Vol. 3: "Peace be Still."* The title track, with its constantly mounting feeling of urgency, was pivotal for gospel, especially as his rough voice challenged the sweetness in the large vocal group behind him. James Baldwin once told his friend Heilbut that just the way Cleveland sang the word "master" was terrifying. "*Peace be Still*" was a huge hit with 800,000 copies allegedly sold, although Cleveland's label, Savoy, was disreputable with numbers.[12] The title song has been covered just as many different ways, although an interesting interpretation came from Giovanni, who recorded it

[11] "James Cleveland: King of Gospel," *Ebony*, November 1968, 74–82.

[12] Bil Carpenter, *Uncloudy Days: The Gospel Music Encyclopedia* (San Francisco: Backbeat Books, 2005), 88.

on her own choir album *Truth is on its Way* shortly before *Amazing Grace.*

"'Peace be Still' always intrigued me," Giovanni said. "Peace being still, rather than peace being busy. Peace as a noun. Peace as a person. I was looking at peace as an entity. He was quoting Jesus. And I was bringing it to the 20th century then. Saying, no, the rumblings of this peace must be still."

Since moving to Los Angeles and forming the James Cleveland Singers in 1962, Cleveland became a gospel industry kingmaker. Within his new city, the gospel audience expanded considerably since the '40s. Jacqueline DjeDje chalks that up to black migration, institutional support among large churches, and more media attention, particularly radio broadcasts.[13] Los Angeles was also the site for an important gospel gathering at the Shrine Auditorium that featured The Caravans (with Cleveland) and The Soul Stirrers (with Sam Cooke); it was captured on the album *The Great 1955 Shrine Concert* (Specialty), another live forerunner to *Amazing Grace.* In 1967, Cleveland established the Gospel Music Workshop of America (GMWA), which had the initial purpose of educating and training young gospel singers, but evolved into a juggernaut through its annual conventions that are

[13] DjeDje, 64–66.

still being held today. The GMWA organizational model followed the National Baptist Convention. Essentially, this made bigger choirs the norm, and Cleveland had them trained to sing as a single instrument. This constituted a major shift in focus for the music from the time Cleveland and Franklin were growing up. Those days featured smaller vocal groups, such as The Caravans, and choirs were not a polished commercial force. As that *Ebony* profile extolled, through the GMWA, Cleveland was "good enough to put together a 300-voice choir within days of arrival at any town." Cleveland turned neighborhood singers into the disciplined Southern California Community Choir in Los Angeles. Archbishop Carl Bean, the city's founder of Unity Fellowship of Christ Church, and a gospel and disco singer knew this since the '60s.

"The voices would be very exact," Bean said. "James was a stickler for clarity around lyrics. I don't care how fast the tempo, with James' choir you heard the words, you heard the parts very clearly and the harmony sitting very well."

Essentially, while Purdie, Rainey, and Dupree made the rhythm section chug and flow with uncanny unison, Cleveland had applied similar methods to the mass choir.

At home in Los Angeles, Cleveland's circle of talented, sometimes classically trained, musicians built their own identities after being a part of his gang — like Billy Preston. Another kid in that clique was Alexander Hamilton, who began writing scores at the age of 6, studied at the Los Angeles Conservatory of Music and Arts, played organ behind Mahalia Jackson, and then joined Cleveland's coterie. When he and I had lunch near the church in which he is pastor, in Compton, it became clear why the leader must have depended on him: along with his prodigious musical skills, Hamilton has the combination of easygoing good humor and dedication that enabled him to thrive in this tough neighborhood. He served as Cleveland's assistant choir director, including on *Amazing Grace*.

As Hamilton says about Cleveland:

> The circle wasn't that big — we all knew each other. Of course, he was already pretty much THE James Cleveland by then. He was in a very interesting position: he had come up through the ranks back East, in the Midwest. And he got a contract with Savoy and it worked great. I think he had eight, ten albums a year he had to do. Way it worked was all he had to do was have his name on it and one song to get paid. Real smart of him — he would look around to the good groups and say, "I'm James Cleveland and will get you on Savoy." We'd do one marathon, six, seven hour session and the album would be done. It would be "James Cleveland

> Presents ..." and he became known as the Star Maker, which put him in a better place than just being the star. Everybody in the country knew that if James Cleveland liked you, he might get you on Savoy, which was basically the gospel music label of the day.
>
> It was sort of fun being one of the king's kids. We got instant respect anywhere we went. He was a nut, but he was fun. You got to be nuts. Especially in gospel because you're not getting paid most of the time. When you look at the field, the genre, and you look at the people doing it compared to the people actually making a living at it, it doesn't exist. He was one of the few who was able to make it, and part of it was by doing the James Cleveland Presents. That made him rich. He was in the right place at the right time. There couldn't be one like him now.

Even during the mid '60s, Hamilton adds that instrumental accompaniment to gospel groups, including Cleveland's massive choirs, was usually minimal:

> It was still, not taboo, but just not done. Drums and the rest of those things in the Baptist churches were just beginning here and there. COGIC churches didn't mind using tambourines, which Baptists did not. Baptists, COGIC to a degree, gospel music people are very conservative. There's a joke, "How many Baptists does it take to change a light bulb?" The answer is, "What do you mean, change?"

Still, Cleveland used drummers on his Savoy records, including a young Purdie who remembers those pre-*Amazing Grace* sessions primarily because of the leader's personality.

"He had his act together, morning, noon and night," Purdie said. "He could raise more money than the Pinkertons. The man just knew what buttons to push on everybody. It was just that good."

All of which made inevitable the ambitious reunion among Aretha and C. L. Franklin, James Cleveland and his Southern California Community Choir, along with Atlantic's top producers and rhythm section.

Chapter Five

Like Purdie said, Cleveland was well on his way to gospel monarchy. Gospel — the music, its message and its audience — had been evolving, too. Major labels, such as Columbia and Atlantic, responded to the market for black gospel that smaller independent companies, like Savoy, had built. By the late '60s and early '70s, gospel artists, like many of their counterparts in soul and r&b, also saw the possibilities of a crossover embrace for their music run up against the reality of segregated audiences. As one of the biggest stars of the day, Aretha Franklin could have towered above all this. For *Amazing Grace*, she plunged back in.

Gospel's rise as a big business, even across racial lines, included the response to the Edwin Hawkins Singers' surprise hit "Oh Happy Day" from 1969. The group, based in Oakland, California, sounded like a looser version of what Cleveland achieved downstate: a choir reworked a centuries-old hymn with funk underpinnings and featured a strong single lead vocalist (Dorothy Morrison). After the song went on Bay Area radio, Neil Bogart of the upstart rock label Buddha signed the group, and its optimistic message reached near the top of the American and British pop charts.

One could speculate on all the reasons why this church song resonated among large white and black audiences while the counterculture and mass movements against the war in Vietnam were gaining steam. A media structure and crossover gospel audience had been building for some time. In 1963 Columbia ran an ad for its compilation of pop-gospel groups recorded at New York's Sweet Chariot club with the tagline, "Can Gospel Replace the Twist?"[1] A few years later, religious-themed music and hippie pop spirituality intersected — like *Jesus Christ Superstar* and George Harrison's ode to ersatz-Hinduism, "My Sweet Lord," which wound up becoming a black gospel standard for a couple of years (usually without its Hare Krishna refrain). Even

[1] *Billboard*, June 1, 1963, 15.

dark psychedelic overlords Funkadelic covered The Gospel Clefs' "Open Our Eyes" in 1969.[2]

But the Hawkins Singers' record's designation at the Grammy Awards showed that a noticeable racial schism still existed within gospel. From 1961 until 1968, the Recording Academy's award in the genre went to either Mahalia Jackson (in 1961 and 1962), or white artists with some country pedigree (such as Tennessee Ernie Ford or Porter Wagoner). In 1968, the Recording Academy introduced a new category, soul gospel (which Dottie Rambo won for "Soul of Me"), that became the de facto black gospel designation. "Oh Happy Day" won that prize the following year — while Wagoner and the Blackwood Brothers took home the best gospel performance award. The divisions continued into the '70s. Looking back, having just two or three separate gospel preferences seems quaint. Today, five categories dividing up the genre at the Grammys, spanning contemporary, rock, rap, r&b, and bluegrass-based gospel.[3]

Major labels, like Atlantic, realized by early 1972 that black gospel albums yielded profits. Wexler's

---

[2] Earth, Wind and Fire recorded this song five years later, but Funkadelic's version had the advantage of Eddie Hazel's blazing, empathetic guitar lines as well as his choir-redolent voice.

[3] grammy.com

company signed the terrific Marion Williams, a veteran of the Clara Ward Singers, and featured the hip Purdie–Rainey rhythm section on her *The New Message* LP in 1969. In January 1971, *Billboard* announced that Atlantic's imprint, Cotillion, would launch a new gospel series and Henry Allen, vice president of promotion, said, "The emphasis of this new series will be on quality gospel recordings and realistic methods of merchandising gospel product."[4] Motown, which briefly had the Divinity gospel division in the early '60s, released a religious compilation *The Key to the Kingdom* in 1971, featuring its stars (Marvin Gaye, The Jackson 5) alongside some white singers (Meatloaf pre-*Rocky Horror Picture Show*). Dionne Warwick stepped away from her Burt Bacharach hits to return to her roots as a member of the Drinkard Singers for her devotional *The Magic of Believing* in 1968, which included a couple of Cleveland tunes. Still, some in the media, during the late '60s, felt that even with such a push, and the star power of gospel-trained performers such as Franklin, the music was unlikely to make major inroads into a white middle-class audience.

---

[4] "Cotillion to Launch a New Gospel Series this Month," *Billboard*, January 1, 1972, 3.

"Its prospects aren't good — no other popular music appeals to so poor an audience," Charles Hobson wrote in *DownBeat* in 1968, "Maybe after the revolution, only a few southern refugees will need gospel. Or perhaps, like blues, gospel will be discovered by young white groups. The Epstein Gospel Singers may be the stars of tomorrow."[5]

At the same time, some felt that since black gospel had forged an uncompromising African American identity, the music should be a source of pride; that maybe the inability to crossover, as Hobson wrote, made the music appealing among cultural nationalists. Although not everyone saw it that way. During the late '60s and early '70s, young composer Richard Smallwood was part of a contingent of students at the historically black Howard University who demanded that the college include gospel in its curriculum. The idea didn't go over well, as the school felt it was more uplifting to reinforce a classical canon.

Smallwood felt that:

> Everything was European classical, which I love, but I wanted to find out more about my culture. We weren't allowed to play gospel in the school of music and

[5] Charles Hobson, "The Gospel Truth," *DownBeat*, May 30, 1968, 20.

> we used to go down into the practice area and have jam sessions, and we'd have somebody as a lookout, stand outside of the door, because if a guard came by and heard us playing gospel, he'd report us and we'd get in trouble with the dean. So I remember we'd jam, play James Cleveland, everyone was singing and somebody would come to the door and say, "Here comes the guard," and I'd break off into Chopin, Bach or whoever, until he passed the room and then I'd go into my gospel jam.

Actually, there had been a protest tradition within black gospel throughout the twentieth century, certainly since Aretha Franklin was growing up in the '50s. Composer Rev. William Herbert Brewster — a favorite of the Ward Singers — used folklore and Biblical scholarship to write such songs of racial uplift as "Move On Up a Little Higher" (echoed in Curtis Mayfield's rallying cry "Move On Up"). An array of lesser-known groups used their songs as direct social/political commentaries: The Ramparts' "Death of Emmett Till," The Gospel Pilgrims' "I'm Grateful to the NAACP," and Otis Jackson's "The Life Story of Madame Bethune." Still, many of the singers and groups who were directly involved in Southern Freedom Riders and other front-line troops in the Civil Rights Movement, like Fannie Lou Hamer and the Alabama Christian Movement Choir, drew more on the earlier Negro spiritual tradition, rather than modern gospel, especially in terms of lyrics and chording.[6]

Black gospel's ideals of pride and empowerment continued during the post-Civil Rights era, even if the lyrics themselves were not explicitly saying so. After all, there had to be more than one cultural counterweight to Richard M. Nixon. The idea that African American religious music, in all its innate rough tones, exemplified the core of racial identity goes back a ways. W. E. B. Du Bois wrote in his 1903 tome, *The Souls of Black Folk*, that, "The Music of Negro religion is that plaintive melody, with its touching minor cadences, which, despite caricature and defilement, still remains the most original and beautiful expression of human life and longing yet born on American soil."[7]

This message resonated slowly within black churches. Theologian James H. Cone's *Spirituals and the Blues* was first published in 1972, although his call to bring liberation concepts to the black

---

[6] Bernice Johnson Reagon collected these recordings for *Voices of the Civil Rights Movement* (Washingto, D.C.: Smithsonian Folkways, 1997).

[7] W. E. B. Du Bois, *The Souls of Black Folk* (New York: Penguin, 1996 edition), 155–156.

church initially didn't have a lot of adherents.[8] Cone argued that Christianity can go hand in hand with black consciousness and that the music from the black Christian church — spirituals, in his example — always expressed a sense of resistance. He takes into account the claims that the lyrics to these spirituals may have actually been coded messages to rebel, or escape to the North. But Cone adds that just through expressing humanity and distinctive views of God, Jesus, heaven, and hell, the spirituals conveyed a liberating message that also came through the blues. Even just saying "I" as affirming a sense of self reclaims an identity that had been stripped from slaves. While his book was published in the same year that Franklin released *Amazing Grace*, he was essentially updating and expanding on the points she raised in her *New York Amsterdam News* column 11 years earlier.

Cone writes:

> So far from being songs of passive resignation, the spirituals are black freedom songs that emphasize black liberation as consistent with divine revelation. For this reason, it is most appropriate for black people to sing them in this "new" age of Black Power. And

[8] Lincoln and Mamiya, 179.

> if some people still regard the spirituals as inconsistent with Black Power and Black Theology, that is because they have been misguided and the songs misinterpreted.[9]

Musicologist Pearl Williams-Jones had been investigating the "distinctly African related traits" in African American gospel around this time. She contends, "The consistent and persistent retention in gospel music performance and practice of a clearly defined black identity growing out of the black experience in America is indicative of the indomitability of the African ethos."[10]

Williams-Jones describes and lists these musical examples, most of which comprise the entirety of *Amazing Grace*, particularly varying vocal tones; emphasis on dynamic rhythms; repetition, and improvisation; communal participation; and a dramatic concept of the music. In discussing how much black gospel singers inherit their style from the discourse of preachers, she cites Aretha and C. L. Franklin as the most prominent example. Cleveland's

---

[9] James H. Cone, *The Spirituals and the Blues* (Maryknoll, N.Y.: Orbis Books, 1995 edition), 35.

[10] Pearl Williams-Jones, "Afro-American Gospel Music: A Crystallization of the Black Aesthetic," *Ethnomusicology*, Vol. 19, no. 3, September 1975, 373.

use of gliding pitches, moans, and wails on "Peace be Still" is her example of the aesthetic beauty in gospel performance that does not adhere to a Western standard.

Conventionally beautiful or not, Cleveland was savvy enough to reflect, and engage, the different ideologies percolating within gospel at the time: commerce on the one hand; cultural awareness on the other. Advertisements for higher-end liquor and fashions fit comfortably alongside the *Ebony* spread about him and his financial achievements. And, as Heilbut reported, he could legitimately address "a group of black militant students at Berkeley" with "thunderous, mildly atonal chords" and the phrase "Right on" in a show of solidarity.[11]

Prominent black ministers were also becoming aware that the messages they were hearing from r&b stars in the latter '60s and early '70s fit with their sermons. C. L. Franklin even openly adopted one of his sermon titles from James Brown: "Say it Loud, I am Black and I am Proud."[12] His daughter made the same proclamation in church without speaking: during the live *Amazing Grace* recording she turns to Alexander Hamilton and they give each other the soul handshake.

---

[11] Heilbut, 219.
[12] Salvatore, 288.

Chapter Six

On the road to *Amazing Grace*, Franklin and King Curtis made a stop further north in California for concerts in San Francisco that would be presented as her, and his, *Live at the Fillmore West* albums, which were recorded during two nights in March 1971. She used Curtis' band, which at that time included Dupree and Purdie. Jerry Jemmott played bass, as Rainey was immersed in New York session work. Franklin and Curtis had become close as he accompanied her on several Atlantic records, particularly *Lady Soul* from 1968. Their pairing sounded like a photo negative of the Billie Holiday/Lester Young voice/sax combination: the former sailed above the beat while Franklin and Curtis dove into it. On the Fillmore West initiation into rock's counterculture, Franklin jubilantly enveloped her vocal pyrotechnics within a new ostensibly laid-back Earth-mother persona.

The high point of the concert and recording was Franklin's duet with Ray Charles on "Spirit in the Dark," which was, by all accounts, spontaneous. Purdie's rapidly syncopated holy-roly beat became more accentuated than it had been on the 1970 album of the same name. In one of Franklin's asides during this Sanctified-inspired performance, she calls Charles "the right reverend." Throughout the concert, she also addresses the audience with the hip "brothers and sisters." And she interrupts the purely sexual "Dr. Feelgood" with a spontaneous, arguably contradictory, spoken sermon about how people can overcome obstacles through faith.

Fillmore West, as well as *Amazing Grace*, included a new band member, percussionist Pancho Morales. Even though conga players were becoming ubiquitous in r&b, Morales is comparatively low in the mix on both albums and doesn't solo, or create any particularly memorable fills à la hip African or Caribbean patterns — or bring Afrocentric percussion to a gospel session. There's a reason for that, which was, as Purdie said:

> Pancho was an alcoholic. It didn't matter what it was, he drank it. Wine most of the time. But he didn't

drink until after the job was finished. But the man would give you the shirt off his back. He didn't have a hurting feeling inside him. He just said what he had to say, he didn't hold things back. He was just a nice guy. That's all he is. Pancho would always play congas like he was the drummer. It didn't matter who the drummer was, he could follow the drummer because he always wanted to be a drummer, so I used to teach him to play drums. No matter what happens, He could follow you right to your grave. He'd blow you out the window, out the door, "You ain't tired yet, come on." Keep you going, motivate you. He always stayed out of the way, but would put the fire under you and you'd have to move. He didn't play around.

Rainey agrees:

How should I say this ... Pancho is a very nice guy. Everybody likes him. He was in your corner, a big, strong in your corner kind of guy. Pancho was not really a musician. Aretha liked Pancho, subsequently being around him we all liked him. A big guy, big ol' strong guy and he does enough as a percussion player. That's about all I can say about Pancho. He carried Bernard's drums. If you ever have a problem with anyone around you, he's got your back. And like I said, once you're in her band, you're there for life.

At least that's how Franklin seemed at the end of *Fillmore West* as she and Curtis were walking off the stage. As the band played the coda to "Reach Out and Touch (Somebody's Hand)," she tells the audience, "Look for King [Curtis] and I to do our thing together for years to come."

The return never happened. On August 14, 1971, as Curtis was carrying an air conditioner to his uptown Manhattan apartment, a junkie blocking his path stabbed him to death.[1] Franklin expressed her sorrow at the loss to Ritz in her memoirs; some, like Atlantic publicist Barbara Harris, suggest that the universally loved Curtis' killing was such a blow to everyone at the company she could see that it would make Franklin more eager to return to the church a few months later. Everybody who worked closely with Curtis considered him a mentor, if not surrogate father, and still can't fathom his murder. As Purdie said:

> I had just talked to him on the phone five minutes before the whole thing happened. And I didn't hear about it until 7 in the morning, when I was coming from Pennsylvania, we were having a party that Saturday night. I was making arrangements and we talked about what he wanted to do. I ran off the road that Saturday morning with the DJ talking about the late, great King Curtis. I pulled over and I was just crying. I just

---

[1] Murray Schumbach, "King Curtis, The Bandleader, is Stabbed to Death," *The New York Times*, August 15, 1971, 38.

> couldn't believe it. The folks watched me, stayed there with me for a good 15, 20 minutes so I could compose myself. Most people don't know the capacity of how I worked for Curtis, what it meant for me. The man taught me the business. I was also his bookkeeper on the road. He showed me how to be a bandleader. He also showed me how to put people together.

Franklin approached Rainey at Curtis' funeral — where she sang "Never Grow Old" — and invited him into the band on a full-time basis. Purdie was recruited as her bandleader the week after the saxophonist's death. Purdie continued:

> That next Thursday was the official time. That was when the job was given to me. [Atlantic executive] Ahmet Ertegun called me first. He called me on Monday and said come by his office. I did and when things were done and finished he said, "You're going to get a call from Aretha and we want you to take the job of musical director. Don't worry about it, Purdie." She called me on Thursday night. I heard five other people they had offered the job to and they said, "The only bandleader you have is Purdie." I mean, they all told me this later. I didn't know how folks felt. But it was Ahmet who told me what was going to happen.

Purdie kept this job for just a few months, including leading up to *Amazing Grace*:

> I'm going to keep it clean. My duties were bandleader. First duties were drummer. Second was front man, third duties were sound man, light man, travel. Then, it comes into conducting. The everything man is the best term that I can possibly give you. What you have to do is when she wants something, you have to stop, do it, and give it to her. The job was a 24 hour job because I was at her mercy for whatever had to be. If she wanted something, she called me. You take the responsibility of the person you're working for. And when you have a superstar, your life is out the window. You're the referee, cut people off at the pass, stop them from getting too close. Then when people want to speak to her, you have to interview everybody. I got called for anything and everything — they couldn't call her. Any call that goes to Ms. Franklin, you had to send them to her music director, so I was getting calls all day and night.

As part of the personal rejuvenation that Franklin described in her memoirs, she and Cunningham took a trip to Barbados where they shot the photo that would become the cover for *Amazing Grace* at Sam Lord's Castle, which had been converted into a hotel. Purdie and Rainey came along for the ride, yet while the bassist recalls her kindness, he added that despite the tours and recordings, she remained withdrawn:

> I was with Aretha for three years and if I were to count the words I heard her say, other than singing,

> it couldn't have been more than 200 words. She very seldom said anything. When she did, she said it hard and quick. Mahalia Jackson was the same way. Sat in the chair with her knees close together, with her arms folded in front of her. Honoring whatever. That was the way she was. I've never been around Aretha where I was, "Wow, Aretha!" I never saw that at all. She would speak to the wives more than to the band.

Rainey does recall one piece of advice Franklin gave him about maintaining focus:

> She came to me one time, I can't remember where we were, and she sat down and said, "Chuck, don't listen to me sing." I was listening to her, you can't help it, she was at the apex of her voice. She knows what she does to the public and didn't want me to get entranced in what she was doing.

It was the sort of input that, if anything, made Rainey even more observant as the group set out to spend a couple weeks in southern California.

Chapter Seven

At some point before, during or after the Fillmore West performance, Franklin decided to return to the church for a different live recording — that much is clear. What remain unclear are all the reasons surrounding the decision. King Curtis' murder following Dr. King's assassination a few years earlier could've given her plenty of reasons to look toward the solace of the church. These weren't the only hardships she would've seen within her inner circle and in gospel itself. Clara Ward and Mahalia Jackson were seriously ill. C. L. Franklin's mounting legal problems included drug charges and the fallout from a deadly gun battle between Detroit police and the militant Republic of New Africa at his church in March 1969.[1]

[1] Salvatore, 291.

Who thought of the record first is debatable: "I told Atlantic that it was time for me to return to my roots and make a gospel album," Franklin told Ritz. "They appreciated gospel and were pleased at my decision."[2]

"I'd been after Aretha from the beginning to return to church and sing the Christian songs closest to her heart," Wexler told Ritz about six years earlier. "The double-LP live album, *Amazing Grace*, was a startling reality."[3]

Who's right? Probably both.

Franklin and Wexler would've known Cleveland's success: Franklin because of their longstanding friendship and mentor–student affinity and Wexler knew how well "*Peace be Still*" had sold. Recording live in Los Angeles would've been equally clear — it's hard to imagine how Cleveland could've captured his choir's energy, feel and intuitive communication after relocating them somewhere near Atlantic's office and Franklin's home in New York. Logistics, the weather, and expenses would've been a strain, too.

The New Temple Missionary Baptist Church in Los Angeles' Watts neighborhood and C. L. Franklin's similarly named church in Detroit were

---

[2] Franklin and Ritz, 150–151.

[3] Wexler and Ritz, 246.

also connected. Their congregants would have had similar backgrounds. By 1972, the area had been notorious for the Watts riots of 1965, yet hadn't achieved any kind of hip underground status from the film *Wattstax*. The church, on Broadway near 87th Street, looks pretty much the same now as it did then. A former movie theater that was converted in 1966, it's by no means a modern mega-church that can hold a few thousand on any given Sunday. It can pack in about 500 for an appearance from a visiting star, like Franklin. Behind the pulpit is a large mural of Jesus Christ's Baptism — which was also there in 1972 — and it depicts Him as more human and burdened than angelic. Outside, the stretch of Broadway appears desolate — some flea market-type stores nearby, that's about it. New Temple itself fulfills a social and economic function in a part of the city that needs it, as much now as 40 years ago.

George Ashford, pastor of the church in 2011, was also a member at the time of the *Amazing Grace* recording. He mentions that C. L. Birden commanded the sort of audience in Los Angeles that C. L. Franklin had in Detroit:

> Pastor Birden had a 6:30 radio broadcast and people would come from all over to be here. He was a

> dynamic pastor, preacher, and teacher and he was also friends with Pastor C. L. Franklin, they were kind of fellowshipping together. Since they were friends, this is a large place and they knew the turnout would be great, so they knew this place would be suited to fit that situation.

C. L. Franklin and Birden were also friendly with Cleveland, and presumably his massive choirs, record sales, and organizational skills would've been enough to forgive the rising gospel star from the earlier infraction that forced him out of the Franklin home. Aretha Franklin was equally enthused about working with her old friend. "James' Southern California Community Choir was one of the best anywhere," Franklin said to Ritz. "I wanted to make this record with James. No one could put together a choir like James Cleveland."[4]

Franklin told Ritz that the preparations for the performance were "intense." Hamilton remembers it differently.

> James just told me one day that we were going to do an album with Aretha, and I said, "OK." That was it. That's basically how it was done. We came to rehearsal knowing what we were going to do.

[4] Franklin and Ritz, 151.

For Purdie, working on this album meant that he didn't have to concern himself with his directorial duties. "*Amazing Grace* was easy because Jerry Wexler was there to take the weight," he said. "I had less to do because everything got filtered down to him before it got to Aretha."

A year before Wexler died of heart failure in 2008, he took credit for having "brought a profane rhythm section into church — it was my idea to get a much more fully fleshed thing." That conversation about the album with his former assistant, Alan Elliott, in 2007 was one of his last in-depth talks about that era. He sounded eager to discuss this album. Wexler was clearly ailing, and kept mentioning his deteriorating condition during their chats. To the producer, *Amazing Grace* represented a perfect combination of the shared high level of technique and dialogue among Purdie, Rainey, and Dupree with Franklin and Cleveland. He then went on to discuss their gospel roots and disconnections with Elliott:

> I got King Curtis' great rhythm section with Chuck Rainey, Bernard Purdie, all the great guys. And what I had them do — this is an interesting point — all black people can refer back to church experience, what they call back in the day, however they were so remote from gospel music that I wanted them to come

> in and rehearse with Cleveland for a few days so they would get the cadence back again. After you've been playing blues and jazz all those years, there's a very subtle difference in the syncopation, harmonies, the fundamentals of how a musician plays. And that paid off because the rhythm section is fantastic. I wanted to really flesh this out.

Wexler was not aware — or, 35 years later hadn't recalled — that Rainey and Purdie had been working extensively in gospel while also recording on r&b and rock sessions throughout the '60s. They would not have forgotten their roots in gospel, or its rhythmic structure. But this was also the first time in a while that Purdie worked under Wexler's co-direction (as opposed to working directly for the musician leader, like Franklin or Curtis) because of an earlier argument. So it's more than likely they didn't have a long discussion about any kind of work. As Purdie said:

> I had been blackballed by Jerry for something that happened in the studio a few years earlier. He made a statement, and his statement was wrong and my answer was wrong. He was trying to say he wanted me to do something like [drummer] Steve Gadd did on a particular record. And it didn't come out that way. He said, "I want you to play like Steve Gadd," And I told

> him, "No, I'll do one better, I'll call Steve Gadd and let him come and do it." He said, "OK, it's done, it's finished." He paid us all and refused to call me for the next couple of years. I was still doing this [work] for Atlantic for King Curtis and so I didn't know this man had fired me. I had never been fired by anybody in my entire life except by Jerry Wexler.

The musicians also included organist Ken Lupper. Another Cleveland protégé, this was the only time that he worked with Franklin's group. Wexler said that his original choice for these keyboard parts was regular Atlantic session player Richard Tee, but chose Lupper immediately upon hearing him. At that time the organist was 18 years old and, as Hamilton said:

> Kenny Lupper — that boy was magical. If Kenny was still alive now, he'd be the Ray Charles of the industry, not that he was blind. Even before Stevie Wonder, the boy was a genius. Wrote some beautiful songs and was very talented all the way around. In playing, singing, writing. He and Billy Preston I would put in the same class. It was his personality. He was just that fun kid who had an infectious way of making you feel good through his music. I don't know how to describe him, other than I just loved being around him. The fresh kid with the smile who just happens to be damn good at what he does — so you loved him, but hated him at

> the same time. Fingers that just fly across the keys and just have a magic when they play.

Rehearsals for the *Amazing Grace* sessions began in late 1971, and were held at Cleveland's Cornerstone Institutional Baptist Church, which was smaller than New Temple Missionary Baptist. The process began with Cleveland, Franklin, and the choir for a few weeks, before the rhythm section joined them. When Franklin described that intensity, she may have been referring to the drills that Hamilton found par for the course.

The Los Angeles-based national black entertainment newspaper *Soul* had its staff on hand during the rehearsals and recording. Its February 28, 1972 issue ran its reports as a cover story with the headline, "Aretha Returns to Gospel." Judy Spiegelman wrote the story, and its co-publisher, Regina Jones, was there to share photo duties, along with Norris Starkey. In the article, Cleveland said that the process had begun the preceding November when Atlantic informed him that Franklin's invitation for them to record together was more than just a friendly gesture. He added that she had been mentioning it to him for years, but it seemed like he never knew that it would actually happen. Cleveland told *Soul*:

> [Aretha] gave me a list of 30 tunes, then her secretary called to add six more, then she called back with four more. Of course she gave me a final list two weeks ago.[5]

Hamilton trained and prepared the choir:

> She and James had gotten together what songs they were going to do and then we spent, I think two, three sometimes four days rehearsing with Aretha. We were sort of putting it together as we went along. I don't know how to do stuff in less than four or five part harmony whereas most gospel people do everything in three. That was what I brought to the table that would not have normally been. Some of the songs, like [Gaye's] 'Wholy Holy' where they wanted to get some of that four or five part harmony flavor, James knew I knew that. Aretha and I would sit and put those things together.
>
> Choral singing is the hardest kind of singing to do. Because it requires precision. In gospel music, we talk about the spirit of God a lot. Some tend to take that moving with the spirit to say you can just do whatever you feel like or go whichever way you feel like going. But choirs that have the discipline will sound better than those that don't. That's why some choirs have spirit — because they have little else. James brought to Southern Cal his knowledge of having worked with

[5] Judy Spiegelman, "After Ten Years Aretha Brings it All Back Home," *Soul*, February 28, 1972, 3.

> choirs, doing this for many years and knowing what works and what didn't. There's a timing to a leader's lead singing, hitting that next note at precisely the moment not only when it carries the message, but cues the background to where they have to go next. Once the music is locked down, so that the sopranos know exactly where the altos are going and very comfortable with what the tenors and baritones are doing, then everybody is free to just sit and James did that with his choir. Some choir directors think that the only way to discipline people is to yell at them and scream at them and such. He wasn't that. Most of the time, anyway.

By the time most of the rhythm section arrived in Los Angeles a few weeks later for rehearsals, the choir had been honed. Rainey and Purdie had been playing the gospel repertoire their entire lives. Purdie adds that the group had recently started performing Marvin Gaye's "Wholy Holy" in Franklin's performances. The drummer's own group — Pretty Purdie and the Playboys, including Rainey and Dupree — released *Stand by me (Watcha See is Whatcha Get)* in the summer of 1971. That album included their own jazz-funk version of Carole King's "You've Got a Friend."

As Dupree recalls by the time the band arrived, the rehearsals were, "soulful, and no pressure put on anyone — straight ahead: you play it, feel it, see where you're going and do your job."

Rainey attests to everyone's hold on the material and adds, "they had two or three Arethas in that choir. They had some ladies who could get it just like Aretha." Still, he contends that there was, "almost too much rehearsal." Rainey continued:

> Too much talking, and, this is a musician talking, too much explanation of this, too much of that. James Cleveland had to make sure everyone understood it was his church, he was in charge. He was trying to protect his ground, but I don't complain about that — it's a thing, we were in Los Angeles and what else are we going to do? You want this to be as good as it possibly can.

At the same time, the bassist noticed that Hamilton seemed to be shouldering a lot of the responsibility during those rehearsals, as Rainey said:

> James would ask Alexander Hamilton to do something here, do something there and it's all about Alexander Hamilton whereas James Cleveland took the credit. Of course, when you spend a week and a half, two weeks with people, you know who they are, they know who you are. You don't remember 30 faces, but you remember the choir director. A choir director basically knows more about music than anybody.

Purdie insists that, in the practice sessions leading up to *Amazing Grace*, Franklin's spontaneity and Cleveland's response threw him. The tapes of these rehearsals have been located in Atlantic's archive and are being prepared for use in the film of the sessions. And like with the version of "Dr. Feelgood" from *Live at the Fillmore West* a few months earlier, Franklin drew on her father's profession. Purdie said:

> The rehearsals were the joint. While we were in the church, Aretha preached. The actual recording of the date was nowhere near like the rehearsal was two days before, the day before. She was actually being a minister. The choir and everyone was in totally in shock because the lady was preaching. She went someplace else. Some of those rehearsals were recorded and he owned them — Jerry did. Man, it was something else. She preached better than any preacher I had been around in years and you felt everything she did. Every song. Every word you were on pins and needles. What James Cleveland would have to say would knock your socks off. He said, "I had never in my entire life had anybody preach better than me." The church, they stood up and looked at him because nobody could believe that coming out of his mouth. It was all spontaneous. They never, in the history of anything that went down, never heard James Cleveland give anybody that sort of praise. Better than him? To him, there was not a preacher in the world better than him.

Chapter Eight

Just before Franklin entered the New Temple Missionary Baptist Church on January 13, Cleveland, her family, Hamilton, and the choir, and guests Clara and Gertrude Ward, had assembled. So did the hundreds clamoring to get inside, even though the event was hardly advertised. Bob Chorush reported in *Rolling Stone* that tickets cost $10 apiece and proceeds were to benefit Cleveland's Cornerstone Institutional Baptist Church.[1] That would be about $52 today, a hefty fee for Watts, but far less than the $17.50 she charged to appear a few month's earlier at Hollywood's Grove ($91 today).[2] Hamilton contends that much of the audience probably paid nothing:

[1] Bob Chorush, "Aretha Sings in a Church in Watts," *Rolling Stone*, April 13, 1972, 22.
[2] usinflationcalculator.com

> Just regular folks. Clara Ward, C. L. Franklin were in the audience. But, just basically, regular church folks who knew somebody to get in. I know I got my mother in. To my knowledge, I don't think they were selling tickets at the door. Most churches, particularly Baptist churches, wouldn't allow anybody to sell tickets. They may have had passes, but I don't recall anybody selling tickets. That was unheard of in the Baptist church. A big, major no-no off the bat.

The cables and microphones leading to the truck in the parking lot would've been no-nos, too — ordinarily. But this crew was as unique as the situation. Wally Heider's company had become the go-to team in the growing field of multi-track remote recording in California, having done such sessions as *Otis Redding Live on the Sunset Strip*. A few months before the session, his company had moved up to a 16-track integrated mobile studio from the standard 8-track.[3] Ray Thompson engineered the *Amazing Grace* session for Heider and arranger/producer Arif Mardin was also in the truck. Wexler seems to be in perpetual motion throughout the film — presumably running from the truck to the church — yet he told Elliott that his role during the recording was limited:

---

[3] Bob Glassenberg, "Studio Track," *Billboard*, July 31, 1971, 4

> There was nothing I really had to do except sit there and be a witness. Remember, these were official church services. I couldn't stop and say, "Let's rehearse those eight bars again." It had to go forward. We didn't stop for anything except if they stopped on their own.

Wexler said he was just interested in "bringing home a good LP master," so he considered director Sydney Pollack's documenting film crew an afterthought. Considering that it was Aretha Franklin, the congregants accepted the movie cameras, lights, and what looks like a scruffy film crew. Hamilton said the choir and the musicians were able to work around them all, as they knew that this was a different sort of situation:

> The one thing that you don't want is for the things with the lights and the director to distract you from doing what you're able to do. He had a camera in the Baptismal pool, behind the choir shooting. Was it OK to do that? Noooo. The good sisters and brothers of the church would have had a cow! Normally, somebody going up there with a camera, they'd be Baptised for real!

Cleveland began both nights with a few opening remarks — Franklin's accomplishments as a singer, and a reminder that, despite the cameras, everyone should be mindful they're in a church. That segued into Lupper's instrumental "On Our Way," as the Southern California Community choir processional entered singing that traditional march. While 35 years later Wexler described the choir wearing robes, they actually looked different. Like with Cleveland's approach to music, the singers avoided a traditional look, but went a little bit further than just modern outfits, or the glamour of the Ward Singers and Gay Sisters. Their uniform of silver vests and black shirts (men and women) looked like they were on loan from Sun Ra. Hamilton said this stemmed from when Cleveland insisted they compete against other choirs, and they had to visually outshine their rivals as much as out-sing them. A Cleveland lesson that Franklin never lost, as her clothes sparkled while striding up the aisles toward the pulpit and she began to sing.

Chapter Nine

While *Amazing Grace* was the finished product of those two January nights when Franklin sang at the New Bethel, it was not supposed to be an accurate presentation of the services. That's to be expected: Atlantic wasn't in the field recording business. Four of the album's songs were repeated on both nights (included on the *Complete Recordings* version). The outro of each service, an instrumental version of Harrison's "My Sweet Lord," was not included on the LP. There were also cuts to what could be called false starts — one with Cleveland laughing as he admonished the congregants for throwing everyone off. He plays piano on most of the album, except for "Wholy Holy" and "Never Grow Old," where he hands off the instrument to his world-famous protégé. Cleveland and C. L. Franklin delivered compelling sermons, which were trimmed for the album. Instrumental and vocal overdubs along with other edits were also part of the finished product. The songs' running order was also reconfigured on the double-LP set, turning *Amazing Grace* into art, rather than merely a document.

"Mary, Don't You Weep"

Amazing Grace begins with a song that Franklin sang toward the end of the second night at New Bethel. "Mary, Don't You Weep" is mostly taken from the New Testament's Book of John (11: 1–45) where Jesus raises Lazarus from the dead before his sisters Mary and Martha. Different versions of the song had been around for a while. The Soul Stirrers recorded "Oh Mary Don't You Weep" (with former member Sam Cooke producing) in 1964, but their traditional take narrated the Israelites' flight from Egypt in the Old Testament (Exodus 14: 1–31). As a nineteenth century spiritual it came loaded with metaphor: Israelites = black people and Pharaoh's army = white pursuers. How these themes resonated among congregants at a Watts church in 1972 could fill another book. The image becomes a framing device for Franklin's version, which adapts Inez Andrews' sermonette with The Caravans. Andrews receives sole composing credit for the song on *Amazing Grace* (rather than, say, "Traditional" or shared "Andrews/Traditional") and royalty checks still arrive in her mailbox.

On the LP, Cleveland's lengthy introduction became abbreviated to the words, "Miss Aretha Franklin." Then the chorus slowly repeats the line "Oh, oh, Mary" with the rhythmic precision that Cleveland's rehearsals instilled. In delivering Andrews' sermonette, Franklin spoke, shouted, and declaimed, without emphasizing the song's melodic line. She also brings in words, phrases from black neighborhoods up front, kind of like the "Sock it to me" refrain in "Respect," the "what it is" in "Rock Steady," or, for that matter, the way she and Hamilton shake hands. This was something that Andrews would not have been able to do in the more conservative '50s. "Mary, don't moan, listen baby, sister don't moan," Franklin ad libbed as she took on the perspective of Jesus relating Exodus to Mary before raising Lazarus. It's possible that His rising from the dead could be taken as a metaphor for calling to arms a people in the turmoil of the early post-civil rights era. Or, it could just be the way Franklin emphasized the name, and the choir and congregants responded. At least that's what struck a young Dianne Reeves, who would go on to become a prominent jazz singer in the '90s. As Reeves said to me:

> It makes you feel like you're standing there watching Jesus calling Lazarus. The thing that really gets me is that in the background, how the choir is very far in the back, like when Lazarus gets up he may be kind of dizzy. You hear these choir members in the background going "woooo, woooo" like that. The way that she sings it, the way that she tells the story, it's almost like you're right there seeing the whole thing go down.[1]

Still, the version on the *Amazing Grace* LP is substantially different from what Franklin actually sang. The sermonette is cut and pasted together so that the New Testament tale is sandwiched between the Exodus parts. These edits still rankle Rainey:

> You got a first verse, second verse, third verse, fourth verse. The musicians inherently will play the second verse based on what happened in the first verse. When they got it back to New York, I remember a situation not too clear, but I remember the gist that Jerry Wexler felt the third verse should be where the second verse is. I'm trying to find a word for that ... you can't do that. He'd come up to me and want something different because I felt, somebody was watching him. On this record, our job as musicians is to be a part of

[1] Reeves also played *Amazing Grace* for Ben Ratliff of *The New York Times*, who included this listening session in his book, *The Jazz Ear* (New York: Times Books, 2008).

> the flow. You don't switch verses, not with that music. It was very, I believe, it was sacrilegious. We played that song a thousand times, I've played it all my life and Aretha has sung it probably all her life. But there's a time to go home and sit down because there are certain people you debate with and certain people you don't debate with. After all, the record was still a hit. And the public didn't know what was going on, but I didn't care for them taking a song and switching verses around.

It's a charge that Rainey has made before, and Wexler had responded to it, but only in the general sense — discussing his role as being at the helm — rather than the specifics of editing this particular song.[2]

"Mary, Don't You Weep" features mostly a 12/8 time signature, similar to the pacing of the Ward Singers' hugely popular "Surely God is Able" in 1950.[3] Still, jazz pianist and church veteran Eric Reed contends that the defining pulse of "Mary" comes every six beats, which would organically make it 6/8. Either way, the rhythm musically announces that this is clearly a gospel album, as it's the beat that

[2] Friedman, "Glory and Injustice," *Dallas Observer*, November 28, 1996 (dallasobserver.com).

[3] Horace Clarence Boyer, "Contemporary Gospel Music," *The Black Perspective in Music*, Vol. 7, no. 1 (Spring 1979), 28.

Purdie discussed as descending from what he called the holy-rolly churches. Another intriguing choice in the sequencing: the song is performed mostly in C#, which is not repeated anywhere else on *Amazing Grace*. Essentially, Franklin sounds bold enough to begin her double-LP set with a song in one of the album's unorthodox keys.

"Precious Lord, Take My Hand/You've Got a Friend"

After "Mary, Don't You Weep," the album moves to Thomas A. Dorsey's "Precious Lord, Take My Hand" — composed 40 years earlier and still one of the most revered gospel songs of all time — blended with Carole King's "You've Got a Friend," from her blockbuster 1971 album *Tapestry*. King had also written Franklin's "(You Make Me Feel Like) A Natural Woman." If Franklin's movement away from the church to pop and back to the church may have turned heads among the faithful, so would reworking "Precious Lord," especially since it was a favorite of Dr. Martin Luther King. Franklin said her reason for doing so was to, "put a pop hit in a gospel framework. It all worked."[4]

---

[4] Franklin and Ritz, 152.

While much of Cleveland's career involved recasting pop songs in a gospel context (he would win a Grammy for his choir's version of Mac Davis/ Elvis Presley's "In the Ghetto" in 1974), Hamilton said that Franklin thought of this blend:

> It was Aretha's idea. She was the one I heard present it. Again, it came naturally. Not about if, it's about how. You'll hear certain things and we worked it out that way.

A big part of what they worked out was Franklin's entrance. Everything sounds built on her, and the band, dropping out and pausing before each line until Cleveland's piano brings them back into the song. It's an ideal tension builder, and, in a bit of irony that's ultimately justified, her improvised call for the congregation to meditate causes them to erupt in cheers. Not hard to understand why her skills cause such adoring reaction. In this medley Franklin flows from E-minor to G to Ab.

Purdie adds that the medley illustrates Cleveland's strengths as much as Franklin's:

> He's taking the top of the lyric and making the choir sing. He was like, "Breathe with me. Come on, breathe." And he'd say certain things and before you

> knew it, a whisper was like a thousand voices. But that's how good the man was. He knew how to work an audience, but he worked the choir the same way.

Duke University African American studies professor Mark Anthony Neal makes an interesting point about this combination in *What The Music Said*. He writes that, "The juxtaposition of Dorsey's composition with King's hugely popular tune implies that Dorsey's marginalized talents are worthy of the same critical attention afforded King, who was arguably the most celebrated popular songwriter of her era."[5]

At the time *Amazing Grace* was recorded, serious studies of gospel music were indeed just getting off the ground.[6] Even today, after Dorsey has been on a U.S.A. postage stamp and such mainstream American icons as Presley have covered his works, he's still not as familiar a name as he should be — even in his adopted hometown of Chicago. So Neal is spot-on in suggesting that Franklin could be implying that

---

[5] Mark Anthony Neal, *What The Music Said* (New York: Routledge, 1999), 83.

[6] Mellonnee Burnim, "Gospel Music: Review of the Literature," *Music Educators Journal*, Vol. 69, no. 9 (May, 1983), 58–61; and Irene Jackson-Brown, "Developments in Black Gospel Performance and Scholarship," *Black Music Research Journal*, Vol. 10, no. 1 (Spring 1990), 38.

he deserves the respect that he lacks to this day. But here's another possibility: the suite combined a landmark song by an African American man with a then-recent pop hit written by a Jewish woman. Maybe this was a feminist statement on Franklin's part. Or maybe her link just emerged from within her own connections.

"Old Landmark"

Franklin's tributes to Clara Ward as she sat in the New Temple pews included an interpretation of the famous Ward Singers' 1951 gospel hit "Old Landmark." Franklin also sang it in the same key (D#) as her mentor. William Herbert Brewster wrote the song and it features his influential compositional techniques, even though the songwriting credit on the album is to "A. M. Brunner." That name was the pseudonym of Savoy Records owner Herman Lubinsky, who released Ward's version. While Lubinsky's scam was typical of early '50s music industry crooks, he was often more insidious than other members of this sleazy class.

"Old Landmark" is built on repeated couplets that an exciting vocalist, like Franklin, transforms through constant shifts in emphasis. This technique works for spoken-word artists, too. As Boyer points out, Dr. King used a similar technique when he repeated "I have a dream" 15 times in his 1963 March on Washington.[7] Brewster spent time with King one day before his assassination.[8]

Franklin and the band also pull off a sleight-of-hand that tripped up even seasoned gospel veterans. Inez Andrews, who notes that "it's hard to get 12 words into one line," added, "I think those lines come in 7/8, 9/10, and 11/12" time signatures. Actually, it's all played in straight-up 4/4, but faster than just about anybody else at that time could sing it. Meanwhile, there was a synchronicity between Franklin's quick phrasing and the double-time Purdie shuffle drum pacing that he picked up from those childhood experiences visiting Sanctified churches.

If there's another layer here, it's in the belief that singing an earlier generation's songs means more than mere nostalgia. Brewster had spoken on the need for black activism and cultural pride years before King and Malcolm X, and he also clarified how his gospel songs conveyed metaphors for civil rights struggles.[9] James H. Cone's ideas of tying messages from the

---

[7] Horace Clarence Boyer, "William Herbert Brewster: The Eloquent Poet," *We'll Understand it By and By* (Washington, D.C.: Smithsonian Institution Press, 1992), 217.

[8] Heilbut, 104.

[9] Heilbut, 98–105.

black church to the consciousness of the times were what Brewster had been saying all along.

A little more than 37 years later, in late June 2009 at the Hollywood Bowl, Franklin sang "Old Landmark," which she dedicated to longtime friend Rev. Jesse Jackson (he was in Los Angeles to assist the family of Michael Jackson, who had died two days earlier). It was the only song she performed that night from *Amazing Grace*, and she introduced it as being from that album — also the only album title she mentioned that night. A year later Franklin performed a few East Coast dates with former piano prodigy/Secretary of State Condoleezza Rice — despite their political and cultural differences (Rice is a Presbyterian, as well as a Republican). In reviewing their Philadelphia concert for *The New York Times*, Steve Smith mentioned the song only in the context of its appearance in *The Blues Brothers*.[10]

"*Give Yourself to Jesus*"

Franklin closes the first side of the album with a song that the audiences most likely did not hear her sing at the church. "Give Yourself to Jesus" was an

[10] Steve Smith, "A Former Secretary of State Has an Audience With yhe Queen," *The New York Times*, July 29, 2010, C3.

instrumental track recorded some time after the mid-January performances and Franklin's vocals were added sometime after that, according to *Amazing Grace* reissue producer Patrick Milligan.[11] The song also foreshadows what would become known as contemporary gospel.

Robert Fryson wrote "Give Yourself to Jesus" (although his version was titled "Give Your Life to Jesus") and his group, Voices Supreme, represented a new musical movement that would arise at the dawn of the '70s and continue to reverberate throughout gospel, which makes its following "Old Landmark" somewhat jarring. This wasn't a traditional gospel song that Franklin would've heard from her childhood musical heroes. Fryson would have been in his late 20s when *Amazing Grace* was recorded. He came out of Cleveland-inspired gospel workshops in Texas. Like his generation's Andraé Crouch, the emphasis was on new composition and a smoother, sweeter delivery than the frenzy of the classic gospel quartets that gave rise to r&b and rock 'n' roll. Some gospel scholars, like Heilbut, believe that this part of Cleveland's legacy made the genre considerably less exciting.

[11] Aretha Franklin, *Amazing Grace: The Complete Recordings* (Rhino) liner notes.

The choir conveys that evenhanded tone, and in a contrast to Franklin's extroversion on "Old Landmark," she sounds restrained here, like she's following the group. She makes some unexpected emphases, like on the line "Give yourself to the master," where her accent is on the sentence's preposition rather than its object. Franklin ends the first side of *Amazing Grace* with a recitation of the Bible's Psalm 23, with its famous line about divine protection while walking through the valley of death. She leaves all inferences — personal, social — open.

"How I Got Over"

The second side of *Amazing Grace* begins with Franklin's interpretation of Ward's 1950 gospel hit, which would have been daunting under any circumstances. But it would've been particularly formidable with Ward and her mother in the pews, although they didn't seem to protest Franklin singing it in a key (F) a step and a half up from Ward (Ab). Franklin performed "How I Got Over" midway through the first night, but according to Milligan the vocals were redone after the church engagements.

Brewster essentially wrote "How I Got Over," although Ward received sole composer credit on *Amazing Grace* because of her new lyrics and arrangement of the song (with Brewster's apparent quiet consent).[12] Either way, the song is as much a standard as any in the American Songbook, even if its performance spaces are primarily churches rather than jazz clubs and concert halls. That influence stretches to The Roots, who used the title, and overt optimism, for a 2010 disc. Franklin's performance on *Amazing Grace* demonstrates how close she was to Ward, especially when compared with Mahalia Jackson's popular version on Apollo from 1951 (or, for that matter, Jackson's version from King's 1963 March on Washington). Franklin's assertive cover of Ward's song acknowledged the influence while it became a vehicle for her to highlight her own identity — much as she did 10 years earlier through her Dinah Washington tribute.

Ward's version and Jackson's couldn't have been more different: Jackson's voice was lower, punctuated with growls, and her overall delivery was strident — conjuring an image of marching just through her delivery. Ward used some melisma, but her higher singing voice was more direct, almost conversational in tone, until she shouts and stretches sidelong

[12] Anthony Heilbut, "If I Fail, You Tell The World I Tried," *We'll Understand It Better By and By* (Washington, D.C.: Smithsonian Institution Press, 1992), 234.

transitional words like "well" and "yeah!" When Franklin sings it, her voice is a bit higher pitched than Ward's, and her lines come across like she's having fun — borne out via her inviting smile on Pollack's film footage. The sense of ecstasy reaches a higher point as she emphasizes the "I" in the title with the shouts that pervade her popular work. Unlike Ward accompanying herself, Cleveland's piano lines drive Franklin and the choir. So does the beat that the rest of the rhythm section plays: Pentecostal by definition, but, it could also be described as funk.

That beat and interplay has fascinated musicians who grew up in a different time and place. A couple decades later, avant-improv drummer Matt Weston listened to *Amazing Grace* while he was studying at Vermont's Bennington College under the late jazz trumpeter Bill Dixon. Weston noted Rainey's lines on "How I Got Over" in particular. He compares him to those of such jazz bassists as Richard Davis, whom Rainey had seen often in New York:

> The upper register-figures on 'How I Got Over' threw me for a loop, and still do when I'm not paying attention. Playing chords was rare, but not unheard of, for an electric bassist, but even that doesn't entirely explain what Rainey's doing. The logic and resolution occur so quickly that it almost sounds like there's a second bassist commenting on what Rainey's doing.

> He quickly ducks into the higher register, sometimes rapidly alternating with lower tones, sometimes not, but never sounds frantic. What's particularly astonishing is at no point is the low end lacking.

Purdie remains just as astonished:

> I wasn't even playing on the first 12 to 16 bars. And when I finally came in, I came in and did what I did because of the figures that Chuck was playing. That's how Aretha wanted it. But I can't say I did that by myself. I got that from Chuck, and I just knew instinctively where to go.

Rainey sounds direct, rather than excited, when talking about his role:

> Well, on songs like "How I Got Over," where you have a good choir, good rhythm section and excellent leader, you just go with what you hear. Being a member of Aretha's band, we were just free. My own church was a family church and my cousins and uncles were musicians and each could wing it in any key and sound like three or four people. Because I played guitar before I played bass, I have a feel for some kind of rhythm in more than one note and that particular album opened up to where I came from. Since I heard that song my entire life, I don't have to think of where the changes are. Just have to hit that G chord when it comes.

"What a Friend We Have in Jesus"

After the twentieth century gospel standard, Franklin moves into the earlier century's hymn "What a Friend We Have in Jesus." The songs flow together, as they're both in the key of F. Like any spiritual, "What a Friend" was frequently performed in churches and so she could have absorbed it from anywhere. But she must have known Roberta Martin's 1950 version with organist Willie Webb, especially considering Cleveland's history with the Roberta Martin Singers. But while Martin sang it as a slow, conversational lament — deliberately dragging out the line about the "needless pain we bear" — Franklin transforms it into a celebration. Purdie simply said it remains his, "all-time favorite song — I knew the song frontwards and backwards: the words, the rhythm that got played, what had to be there."

In the film footage, the choir sings while sitting (none of the synchronized stomping that has become the usual image of gospel performance). So it makes the build-up to Franklin that much more dramatic. Especially when Cleveland jumps up from the piano to shout, "Sing it!"

Along with the title track and "God Will Take Care of You," "What A Friend" was one of the three songs on the record that had been published in *Gospel*

Pearls. Hamilton said that for this performance he simply wrote an arrangement around the basic chords he took from the hymnal to lend more space to the chorus. He added that Franklin's direct way of singing the name in the title may have become lost in contemporary gospel:

> One of the things I've noticed in recent music is that there's too much icing and not enough cake. A friend of mine asked, "When did gospel go baroque?" There's just one word: Jesus. Not Jeeeessssuuuuuuuuss all over the place. A real artist like Aretha knows when to do and when to not. She knows when less is more, when more is more. Her and those like her had been in the trenches. You don't see a lot of that these days.

Franklin also plays celeste on this song, which she had played on a recording once before ("All the King's Horses" on *Young, Gifted and Black*), and not much afterwards. The instrument adds a different texture, but ultimately seems superfluous alongside Dupree and Rainey.

"Amazing Grace"

Almost 11 minutes long and free from any such restraints as set meter, Franklin threw everything into the British-hymn-turned-multiracial-American-church-standard that became her album's title track. She made the version stand out in a crowded field.

Steve Turner's 2002 book *Amazing Grace* tells the story of the song and lyricist John Newton, who actually never quit slave trading. Turner writes that while "Amazing Grace" was recorded infrequently before 1971, that changed during the early '70s and "of the 457 commercially released recordings held by the Library of Congress, 97 percent were made between 1971 and 2001."[13] Turner credits the change in its acceptance to the pop counterculture's newfound embrace of religious themes, describes in detail Judy Collins' version from *Whales and Nightingales*, and discusses Franklin alongside the Royal Scots Dragoon Guards' bagpipe rendition. Yet Franklin's superior range and improvisational brilliance give her ownership of the song.

Turner states that Franklin reduces the melody and lyrics of "Amazing Grace" to two stanzas that she stretches to an 11-minute performance. While she did reshape the structure of the song, everybody has somehow reworked it. The five stanzas in *Gospel Pearls* are not the six that Newton wrote. And, as Hamilton said, "Aretha can do that song 100,000

---

[13] Steve Turner, *Amazing Grace* (New York: Harper Perennial, 2002), 178.

times and never duplicate that exact performance. When you get in front of the audience, even the audience will change what you were going to do. That is what makes gospel music gospel music."

What makes it Franklin's gospel music is her extraordinary sense of control. She begins with a hum and eases into the song gradually following the choir. Just about every vowel is extended, but then she'll cut them all as she delivers the line "been right here in the midst" as a sort of proto-rap. The colloquial "right on" and "oh, yeahs" are not only the improvised interjections that Turner notes, but are stacked toward that easily identifiable gospel shout at the end of the song.

Australian music professor and choir director Andrew Legg has written that "Amazing Grace" shows how Franklin and Mahalia Jackson employed a similar technique that he identifies as a "closed-mouth moan" — strangely, he doesn't mention Ward's influence. Nor does he mention the legendary Philadelphia soprano Mary Johnson Davis, who also inspired Franklin. The comparison he makes is to Jackson's recording of "The Upper Room." Legg writes that technique is used to punctuate the different parts of the songs.[14] This much is true, but

[14] Andrew Legg, "A Taxonomy of Musical Gesture in African

then he likens this moan to a cry of physical pain. Franklin's uplifting tone contradicts that description.

If the image of Franklin singing "Amazing Grace" is one of fervid divine inspiration, orderly symmetry was engineered in post-production. This song, which closes the second side, and "Give Yourself to Jesus" at the end of the first, both are mostly sung in the key of Ab. It makes for a cogent parallel, but Purdie still hopes for an earlier version's release:

> I'm sorry that the people never heard "Amazing Grace" from the rehearsal. The rehearsal was better than what was put on the record because the lady preached. After she had done the song, she preached, and then she came back into the song.

"Precious Memories"

With the traditional "Precious Memories," Franklin begins the third side of *Amazing Grace* like the ending of *Live at the Fillmore West*, in a duet with a strong male counterpart. And similar to her pairing with Ray Charles, Franklin sings back-and-forth lines with Cleveland rather than their blending together. All of which works for a number of reasons: the

---

American Gospel Music," *Popular Music*, Vol. 29, no. 1 (2010), 106.

call-and-response dynamic between preacher and congregation being the most obvious. But there's also a fun contrast here: Cleveland's a raspy baritone and Franklin is most decidedly not. His own drawn-out timing echoes the mighty Robert Anderson, who had sung with The Caravans. At that same time, Franklin and Cleveland bring similar techniques to the performance. Both use ad-libs and those close-mouth moans, especially when Franklin delivers her "mmm-hmmm" in response to Cleveland's shout about Jesus' presence when "every, every now and then you're going to get a little lonely."

Although Franklin could've heard the traditional song anywhere on the gospel circuit, she could not have avoided Sanctified proto-rock virtuoso guitarist Sister Rosetta Tharpe's hit version from 1948. Tharpe's crossover from an insular church to international stardom differed from Franklin's journey, although the guitarist's format on this song did help establish a precedent. Just as jazz musicians accompanied Franklin on her early Columbia recordings — and a jazz-inspired group worked with her on *Amazing Grace* — boogie-woogie pianist Sam Price's trio backed Tharpe on her "Precious Memories."

The track's position on *Amazing Grace* reinforces the album's musical symmetry. "Precious Memories," which starts side three, is in D#, which — like the opener "Mary, Don't You Weep" in C# — is a key never repeated on the album. Also, both "Precious Memories" and "Mary, Don't You Weep" share a fairly distinctive time signature. Even though "Precious Memories" sounds like it's in 3/4, jazz pianist Eric Reed contends again that the pulse may be more of a 6/8, as is "Mary." These tempos are similar, but, either way, they provide a deliberate-sounding beat that lets Franklin soar.

In her memoirs, this was the only song on *Amazing Grace* that Franklin mentioned in terms of its lyrics, saying only, "precious memories is what the service was all about."

"Climbing Higher Mountains"

After the lengthy "Precious Memories" (and "Amazing Grace"), there's a segue into the shortest song on the album. Gospel scholar Bob Marovich suggests it's possible that Franklin heard "Climbing Higher Mountains" from Alex Bradford's former group, The Willie Webb Singers, who recorded it for Parrot in 1953; it didn't sell much, but they could've performed it at Detroit revivals that she may have attended. The two-and-a-half-minute song is a straight shot back to the blues: as with other overtly blues-tinged songs on *Amazing Grace*, it's in F. But that impression is also felt because Dupree's Texas-derived sliding vibrato sounds particularly clear on this one. Franklin begins singing it in a blues tonality as well. Then Dupree, Rainey, Purdie, and Lupper turn the beat around, ramping up the tempo while still keeping everything in a most basic 4/4. And that, in turn, causes Franklin to stretch to an upper tier of her range to hit the word "higher." Which she nails.

It would be easy to read an underlying message of this song. As with almost every line on the album, the song adds up to a positive message resonating during a crossroads in the immediate post-civil rights era — a long way from when teenage Franklin recorded "There is a Fountain Filled With Blood" and its image of sacrifice. Hamilton, though, is reluctant to assign recording a song like "Climbing Higher Mountains" to any particular point in time. As Hamilton said:

> The words are from old spirituals, we are climbing Jacob's Ladder. You're taking words in gospel from the Bible, so there's only so many basic subjects you could have. Most old spirituals were about going to the promised land, getting up from here to there, or going to a better place or just get through this one. Or trusting God to get you from here to there.

Remarks by Reverend C. L. Franklin

When C. L. Franklin spoke toward the end of his daughter's two-night stand at the New Bethel Missionary Baptist Church it was one of the "occasional brilliant bursts" of light at a time when "his power continued its inevitable decline," according to Nick Salvatore.[15] Still, he sounds confident and strong here, which is a two-minute selection culled from his longer sermon. The essence is: Franklin says that daughter Aretha "is just a stone singer" and "you want to know the truth, she never left the church." He also talks about how emotional he felt at seeing her sing with her childhood friend Cleveland again.

There could've been numerous reasons for including C. L. Franklin's speech before the last quarter of the album — as opposed to its actual placement as, basically, the penultimate track. Maybe to ensure that *Amazing Grace* buyers wouldn't skip over the spoken words. Or, possibly, as Aretha Franklin's phrasing owes much to her father, it was about maintaining the familial flow.

[15] Salvatore, 298.

"God Will Take Care of You"

"God Will Take Care of You" goes back to the early twentieth century (credited as a traditional on *Amazing Grace*, and by C. D. Martin in *Gospel Pearls*), and, most likely, it derives from an older spiritual. In the early '50s, the song became a hit single for the Gay Sisters, selling 100,000 copies according to some sources, but definitely not profiting the actual singers, according to the youngest Gay Sister, pianist Geraldine, and their younger brother Donald.[16] The Gay Sisters' version of the song would've been the one that Franklin heard on the circuit, and Cleveland would've been well aware of it because of his affinity for the family.

Horace Clarence Boyer mentions in *The Golden Age of Gospel* that vocalist Mildred Gay and singer/ pianist Evelyn Gay transformed the hymn "from the somber and lifeless performance usually given it to a rollicking 12/8 song of conviction and assurance."[17] More specifically, *Gospel Pearls* had set the tempo of this song as 6/8, and while the Gay Sisters' performance is ostensibly quietly straightforward, the beats associated with the Sanctified church rumble beneath them.

---

[16] The sales number is cited in Carptenter's *Uncloudy Days*, 150.
[17] Horace Clarence Boyer, *The Golden Age of Gospel* (Urbana, IL.: University of Illinois Press, 1995), 243.

Franklin and her group transform the song yet again, with the rhythm at a slower 9/8, the only song on the album with this time signature. But they also make explicit the Sanctified shout that the Gay Sisters imply. It's a full-throated performance filled with the ad-libs that Franklin had been revealing throughout the album. It's also the point on the album where Cleveland tells the Baptist audience that they'll be moving into the rhythms of the Sanctified church. With Purdie and Rainey underpinning the foot stomping, hand clapping, shouting coda. Although such inter-denominational meetings are not unheard of, to point them out on a major-label recording has always been considerably rare.

"*Wholy Holy*"

While Franklin ended side three visiting a hit from the golden era of post-World War II gospel, she began the final side of *Amazing Grace* with a song seemingly from the secular side of the era's soul-gospel hybrids. Sanctified minister's son Marvin Gaye's "Wholy Holy," and much of its surrounding *What's Going On*, could've fit alongside a religious music program. It was one of the few Motown-affiliated songs that Franklin released on Atlantic, although she dipped into her Detroit neighbors' repertoire throughout her career.[18] Franklin selected this song quickly: Gaye released *What's Going On* about eight months before the *Amazing Grace* sessions, and since Purdie said that they had been performing "Wholy Holy" as part of Franklin's gigs for a while, that would've been right at the time Gaye released his album. "Oh, gosh, she just loved that song," Purdie said. "And for us, we just basically had to follow her."

Franklin and Gaye had the most distinctive voices in popular music at that time: his range being just over three octaves and hers at three and a half. Both were uncanny stylists who created the template for generations of followers. They approached his song absolutely differently.

Gaye's wistfully sings "Wholy Holy" as if he were looking downward, offering the lasting image from the line, "Jesus left a long time ago, said he would return." Franklin, sitting at the piano, shouts His name, and her approach is as earthy as Gaye's was airy. Although the main difference is the line she emphasizes: "People we've got to come together." And the "we've" was her interjection. Those words

[18] Franklin recorded her version of the Gaye/Tammi Terrell duet "You're All I Need to Get By" as a single that was released on February 3, 1971. She also performed Nicholas Ashford and Valerie Simpson's "Reach Out and Touch (Somebody's Hand)" on *Live at the Fillmore West*.

could be as significant as her call for respect five years earlier. In the years after Dr. King's assassination and continued urban unrest, unity became all the more necessary. The improvised line about everyone "movin' and groovin' with love" in this context may or may not be interpreted as a communal approach to appreciating the divine.

Unlike Franklin and her group, Hamilton didn't previously know Gaye's song. That gave him the freedom to come up with a unique arrangement:

> Since I had never heard Marvin Gaye do it before we started working on it, I came into it fresh. Aretha played it and said, "OK, how can we do this for the chorus?" The chords in the background are mine. I heard the five notes, as I recall AbMaj7 with the bass, actually made it an Fmin9. An AbMaj7 over an F, which makes it an Fmin9. Those were the chords that I heard the pianist do, so I transmitted those and had the choir do them. So when we started singing it, it made it a whole different kind of a sound of a song. Again, I hadn't heard the original, so to me, this was cool. The way we should do it. No big deal. It's a big deal now listening to it vis-à-vis Marvin Gaye's version, but I hadn't heard it back then.

"Wholy Holy" is also the first song on *Amazing Grace* that features Franklin on piano. Her opening lines illuminate what Herbert Pickard said about her style differing from Cleveland's. Rather than unleashing the sort of strong, mid-range chords for propulsion, she uses lighter, higher-register single notes as framing for her entrance. She is also a smart enough instrumentalist to choose seemingly delicate notes that subtly enhance her own forceful vocals. In other words, she made the piano resemble Gaye's voice.

"You'll Never Walk Alone"

Franklin sang "You'll Never Walk Alone" on the first of the two nights at New Temple Missionary Baptist, even though it's the penultimate song on *Amazing Grace*. Sung early during the run, some technical problems with the recording meant that she recreated much of it later on in the studio (why she apparently didn't seem to repeat it the following night is unknown). The way the chorus comes in suddenly also attests to piecing together bits in the studio. But its place on the record just after "Wholy Holy" offers a sense of continuity with some pronounced modulation. Even though Franklin re-recorded her lead vocals, the choir in both songs sang Hamilton's five-part harmony arrangements with the previous song in Bb and "You'll Never Walk Alone" one whole step back in Ab. As Hamilton said:

> There's one song that you never would hear in gospel services. I don't think I'd ever heard it done in a Baptist church. Aretha wanted to do it. So, Aretha gets what she wants. If they're paying, you play what they tell you. That whole ending with the chords, those are mine. Five part harmony thing. She has said this is what we're going to do, just do it.

The song comes from the Richard Rodgers and Oscar Hammerstein musical *Carousel*, the film version of which was released in 1956, around the same time that Franklin made those initial recordings in her father's church. While it never became part of a musical liturgy, Mahalia Jackson recorded it for Columbia and sang it on her late-night television broadcast. Clara Ward sang it, too. Still, it would be futile to trace Franklin's inclusion of this song to any one source, considering how she grew up hearing Judy Garland with one ear, even if the other was tuned to Dinah Washington and Ward. And Franklin's reshaped other songs from musicals and turned them into testimonials, like when she sang Mitch Leigh and Joe Darion's "The Impossible Dream" at Rosa Parks' 2005 funeral in Detroit.

"Never Grow Old"

Critic Will Friedwald contends that Franklin's music "preaches the gospel of optimism" and while her first name is one letter shy of an anagram for Earth, she "embodies an underlying message of heavenly hopefulness."[19] He refers to her popular hits ("Natural Woman," and "Respect"), although a number of her lesser-known, equally convincing, songs contradict this description — "Dark End of the Street," and "River's Invitation" being two examples. "Never Grow Old" being another.

Casting "Never Grow Old" in a less-than-sunny perspective comes from the first time Franklin recorded it at the age of 14 in her father's church. She mentions in her memoirs that she first heard Samuel "Billy" Kyles perform it with the Thompson Community Choir, although a more likely source was Kyles' version that was released as a single with the Maceo Woods Singers.[20] The spirit inside the traditional "Never Grow Old" comes from the New Testament's Revelations 21: 4 about a vision in which

---

[19] Will Friedwald, *A Biographical Guide to the Great Jazz and Pop Singers* (New York: Pantheon, 2010), 183.

[20] Unfortunately, this Vee-Jay hit is not included in the Shout! Factory box set. Neither is Woods' popular mid '50s instrumental version of "Amazing Grace."

God will put an end to death itself. An uplifting thought, but underlying it is the notion that the world remains nowhere near that heavenly kingdom. Also, this passage in Revelations comes after the dust has settled onto this world. The performance was of a piece with the dark religious songs she sang as a teen, like "There Is a Fountain Filled With Blood," and "While the Blood Runs Warm." Still, the theme of a better world somewhere out there runs throughout gospel — the Flying Clouds of Detroit's "When They Ring Those Golden Bells" from 1957 being one example — and secular music. After all, another Franklin hero, Judy Garland, made a name for herself with "Over the Rainbow."

Naturally, the 14 year old Franklin who sang and played piano on "Never Grow Old" in Detroit sounded markedly different from the almost 30-year-old who performed it in Watts. Back in 1956, Franklin played the sort of rumbling chords associated with Cleveland. She started haltingly and then shouted and repeated the word "old" while the congregation cheers her on: it's a furious performance for anyone, especially a singer too young to drive. Yet in the nearly 10-minute version on *Amazing Grace* (15:27 on the *Complete Recordings*), she reaffirms how much she absorbed throughout her entire career. In 1972, Franklin's phrasing was sculpted, she knows how to quietly stretch out phrases, improvise spoken lines and use moans for punctuation. Essentially, she put all she learned into creating a feeling of tension. With the instrumental accompaniment being just herself and Lupper's organ, this is where the latter's performance illustrates what Hamilton and others said about his talent. He knows precisely where and when to break in with, and hold, his single note lines in response to Franklin's right-hand fills.

Franklin has sung "Never Grow Old" often at funerals — including King Curtis — and there's a YouTube clip of her performing it in memory of Bishop David L. Ellis in 1996 at the same Detroit church where Rosa Parks' funeral would be held nine years later (reaffirming not only C. L. Franklin's claim that his daughter never left the church, but stayed close to certain particular churches). Her range is less than it had been 34 years earlier, and, understandably, that childhood heft is long gone. But what's most clear is the way she controls every note. Just like in the film of *Amazing Grace*, she beams.

At the end of the recording sessions, everyone just packed up and went their separate ways. On the film clip, the congregants casually walk out of the church, around the musicians while they're playing the "My Sweet Lord" outro. But one immediate emotional reconnection took place in the shadows: Purdie and

Wexler reconciled after the drummer's dismissal over the Steve Gadd incident.

"After we did *Amazing Grace*, it was an 180 degree turn — the respect for each other was there," Purdie said. "We talked about it, and I said, 'I didn't know you had fired me. He said, 'You know what, I thought that.'"

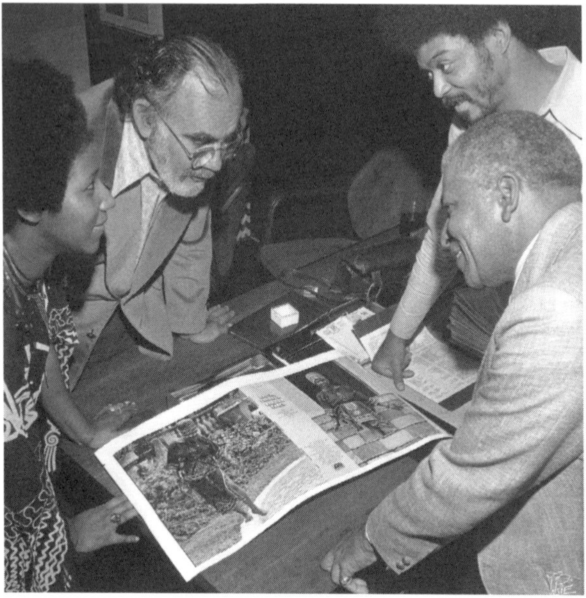

Aretha Franklin (from left), Jerry Wexler, Atlantic executive Henry Allen, and Ken Cunningham assess the cover art to *Amazing Grace*, May 1972.
Credit: Photo by William "PoPsie" Randolph (© 2010 Michael Randolph)

Chapter Ten

A couple of months after Aretha Franklin spent two nights recording *Amazing Grace*, she showed up at Atlantic studios to see Arif Mardin for remixing and editing. Mardin's son Joe recalls that she trusted his father's musical judgment, and with good reason. Of all the higher-ups at Atlantic, he had the most extensive background and training as a composer and arranger. Mardin (alongside Tommy Dowd) was also one of the first to delve into recording up to eight tracks back in the late '50s. All of which became important when Franklin asked him to help her re-record "You'll Never Walk Alone."

"She didn't like one part of the song, so she came to the studio and played it and sang and said, 'Make your edit there,'" Mardin told Tom Doyle for the British magazine *Sound on Sound* in 2004. "I said,

'How are we gonna make an edit into the live church sound?' So I assembled a lot of people and they would talk and hum and clap and everything to create that atmosphere. Then I took a room murmur of the church and made a long loop out of it. On the splice, I put a cymbal and things like that and it worked out fine."

Along with reworking the song order, a few other tweaks were made in the studio: a common practice for concert albums. Assisting engineer Jimmy Douglass said that Franklin's frequent backing group, The Sweet Inspirations, may have added some overdubbed harmonies, but he's not certain (he was a teenager at the time). It's also possible that the backing vocalists were her sisters, Erma and Carolyn, and cousin, Brenda Corbett. More strings were added to "Wholy Holy," which was one of the album's few misguided aesthetic choices — Dupree's guitar part was more than sufficient. Overall, though, engineer Gene Paul (then in his early 20s) said that the generally loose, hands-off, attitude toward mixing *Amazing Grace* exemplified what made the overall sound of these Atlantic LPs stand out from Franklin's earlier label. This approach contrasted to eight years earlier when Atlantic heads considered the idea of recording and selling a Dr. Martin Luther King, Jr. sermon, but dismissed it as the live response from his church audience would mar the sound quality.[1] As Paul said:

> Mixes have a lot to do with the calling of how it was performed. That's the first thing. Second thing is how it was recorded. All of these things together multiply themselves and come out to what the mix is, unless you force it. And those mixes were not forced. Those mixes were as comfortable as if the Lord shined down and said, "This is how we do it. You got one mic, do your act." Nothing was done technically perfect because the minute you make it do something it wasn't supposed to do, you change the whole scope of it. And they were all such professionals, or novices, whatever they were, that's the only place they played because they owned it. They couldn't do a Columbia version if they wanted to. I couldn't do something clean as a whistle and sterile as hell. Nobody was fighting to be something they wish they would be. They all did something that they owned and that's part of the magic why Atlantic was who Atlantic was.

That homegrown sensibility extended to the album's outer packaging, which featured Ken Cunningham's shot of Franklin in Barbados — sitting regally on the front, casually dipping a toe in the pool

---

[1] Brian Ward, *Just My Soul Responding* (Berkeley, CA: University of California Press, 1998), 272.

on the back. In both photos, the focus is on Franklin's crimson gown and matching turban, which made her appear closer to such cultural advocates as Nina Simone or Abbey Lincoln than any of her peers in r&b or gospel. The jewelry that adorned Franklin in the early '60s was gone — as were the sequins when she sang at New Bethel in 1972. Even if dashikis and afros were the styles of the street, Franklin was one of the only black female pop stars to publicly embrace the look on the cover of her commercial product. On *Amazing Grace*, the direct shot of Franklin exends the image inferred on *Young Gifted and Black*. Franklin's fashion sense was ahead of her time as much as a part of the zeitgeist. Example: about 40 years later, Attallah Shabazz, daughter of Malcolm X, wore a similar dress in a New Yorker photo spread on civil rights leaders and their descendants.[2] But back then, Franklin's friend Nikki Giovanni found the look to be familiar, and adds that cultural solidarity didn't mean a downscale price:

> She looked good, didn't she? She's kind of putting her toe in, Baptised. There was a shop in New York called Ashanti. I'm sure she got it from Sandy who

[2] Platon, "Portfolio: The Promise," *The New Yorker*, February 15 & 22, 2010, 109.

> designed for Ashanti. To see Aretha in an Afrocentric dress was the right thing because she's an African princess, as it were. It looked good and she looked comfortable, there was joy. The store started off in Harlem, but they moved down to Madison Avenue because Afrocentric clothing became in for a while. Mostly cloth, because they made it. So they had very little ready to wear. If you wanted something, you went in and talked to Sandy. In four weeks you could have your dress. I'm sure they made more than one for Aretha, because she was right there. It was nice, what they did in the '60s, incense burning with the candles, you could drink tea. Everything you'd have in an upscale shop. It was never cheap.

Franklin didn't limit wearing the gown to a vacation, or posing for the album cover, as shown in William "PoPsie" Randolph's photo of her at an Atlantic executive meeting. This image also reaffirms that Franklin's involvement in the album's production went beyond singing and song selection. Production credit is an empowering statement for an artist, especially a black woman: even big rock bands, like the Rolling Stones, usually didn't get named as co-producers at that time (although Franklin's labelmate Jimmy Page did). But what's also striking about the picture is Franklin's divided attention: her clear excitement may be from seeing the cover art to the album for the first time, or maybe it just reflects how she and Cunningham felt about each other. Either way, everything about *Amazing Grace* added up to a personal celebration.

That jubilant spirit would have been capped had Pollack's film of the recording been released at the time. Originally, Warner Brothers had intended to release the film as part of a blaxploitation double-feature with *Superfly* — a juxtaposition that makes little sense, especially since a pairing of *Amazing Grace* with *Wattstax* instead would've better defined the era than any other four hours. The studio wound up just shelving the project and Pollack became so busy as a director and actor during the next few decades, he didn't have an occasion to look back on those two days. Alan Elliott, a former Atlantic producer, started asking his friend Wexler questions about the footage around 2007. Along with business partner Herb Jordan, they acquired the rights to edit and release it in 2008, and discussed the completion with Pollack before his death that year. Elliott and Jordan's endeavor became public in a January 2010 article in *Variety*.

Franklin has expressed ambivalence about the film. In her memoirs, she says, "I believe I said God is good, and if a movie were meant to be, it would happen." But along with saying that there was no agreement in place for her performance to be filmed, she adds that she was appalled that "one of the cameramen kept shooting straight up underneath Clara [Ward's] dress. She was in the front row. Talk about bad taste!"[3]

That shot is not in any of the footage I screened.

[3] Franklin and Ritz, 153.

Chapter Eleven

Amazing Grace hit the stores on June 1, 1972. Initially, no singles were issued in advance of the album, although "Give Yourself to Jesus" b/w "Wholy Holy" came out 6 weeks later — after the LP had been selling steadily. By the early '70s, the move away from an emphasis on one-shot 45s to thematically unified LPs had gradually been taking hold in soul music, as it already had in rock: Gaye's *What's Going On*, Curtis Mayfield's *Curtis*, and Roberta Flack's *Quiet Fire* being three examples. In some regards, Franklin fit right in with this group, not only because Rainey and Purdie also played on Flack's record. *Amazing Grace* included Franklin's take on Gaye's recent work, but her consciousness-raising inferences and extended songs echoed her contemporaries' statements. Still, in a marketplace that acknowledged

Franklin's momentous hit singles, selling her as an album artist would've been difficult. Especially when there were articles such as those in a January 1972 *Billboard* that attributed Atlantic's 10 percent sales hike to her "12 gold singles, the highest ever for a female artist."[1] So the company's strong marketing team took different paths in promoting the album.

During the late '60s, the company hired more African Americans in executive a&r (artists & repertoire) and promotions roles. The move may have been in response to such incidents as threats made against Wexler, who was seen as a white parasite when he attended the National Association of Television and Radio Announcers convention in 1968, to accept an award on Franklin's behalf from the black media organization.[2] It was also sound business sense to hire such pros as Barbara Harris and Walter Moorehead.

Harris joined Atlantic in 1969, and she had previously worked with Franklin's longtime agent and confidant Ruth Bowen at Queen Booking. For the most part, Harris remembered that publicizing *Amazing Grace* was, "straightforward — setting up releases, trying to get print interviews and all that." She says a problem was that, "Aretha was kind of

---

[1] "Atl. Claims 10% Sales Hike," *Billboard*, January 15, 1972, 4.
[2] Wexler and Ritz, 227–228.

reserved, but nice and quiet. Introspective, I guess. She's not a loudmouth by any means today, but she protects herself more. You couldn't get Aretha to do but so much press. You couldn't have her out there every day doing interviews and blah, blah, blah. But given who she was and that the album was so fantastic, people really pulled the stops out."

Part of that promotion included bringing Franklin back into churches, according to Harris. She adds that, along with visiting a lot of churches herself, C. L. Franklin's influence also helped spread the word.

Moorehead took a different approach. A New Orleans native and Vietnam veteran, his job was to get radio airplay throughout the South. He said that the era's pressures on him being a black record company man who often had to work in a still-segregated white region, "was like an elephant sitting on my testicles." Not that having to promote an album by a prominent artist without digestible 2- or 3-minute singles made his job any easier:

> She was really hot when the album came out. I was kind of upset — because with all her singles that she came out with, albums weren't that prevalent at the time, you move 150,000 units and it jumps to the ceiling. So I had to come up with a scheme to get that done because the album was absolutely monstrous. Also, she had this African attire on and the black

consciousness movement was in progress, so it made it a little easier to go to black radio. Pop, I didn't see a chance with that. First of all, with that attire, a white boy don't want to hear about that. At that time, things were still tough down here in the South. Normally, you see white guys with that rebel flag on their license plates, they could do that. But if I would come up with a dashiki on, like she had on, they would take offense at that and would not allow you to excel. That meant I had to push hard on r&b stations, not just gospel. They had a full gospel program on the major r&b stations. That's how I was able to make this thing happen. At night, midnight until 6 in the morning, I would give the jocks their product so they wouldn't have to pay for it. In turn, I'd say, "play this cut" or "play that cut late tonight." I had them play the *Amazing Grace* cut, as they were getting ready to get off, they would segue out with Aretha into the morning show. Then the morning show takes off, waking people up with r&b music. So that's how things happened with that record and I did that with every city that I had to work.

When Alexander Hamilton talks about first seeing what he calls the "very avant-garde" look that Franklin promoted on the cover of that album he helped work on, he raises an eyebrow in a look that blends mild astonishment with admiration:

We hadn't been African Americans for very long in those days. When I was a kid in the late '40s, early

> '50s, the word 'black' was a word we used in the neighborhood as an epithet. It would get you hurt. If an African American called another one black, they'd be ready to fight. Black is Beautiful was a shock term, and that's why they used it. They were turning the word around. So when Aretha came out with this and was wearing the whole dashiki, it was big. Nobody threw it out, because it was Aretha, but they went, "I don't know." But then they bought the album. It's just that she was wearing something that was not exactly church clothes in those days. But, again, it was her. To many church folks, we just loved Aretha and she can do no wrong.

As Hamilton said this, he offered another reason why Franklin received acceptance from the church, even after she crossed over to become a worldwide star singing gospel-infused secular songs. He contrasts her decisions with Clara Ward and her sisters, who received scorn among the faithful for a gospel program at Disneyland:

> By Clara doing the show, that hit right on time, meant they had to do it by script. So they had a very canned presentation. A good presentation, but canned. Which, to the black community, it was not real. If it's by script, how can it be by spirit? So she was playing church and that's a big no-no. Aretha didn't do a gospel show anywhere else, she kept the separation there, so

> the church people could accept her for coming home and doing her gospel here, because she didn't do it out there. That made it different than it might have been otherwise. Nobody hated her for what she did, because she kept it pure. She wasn't using gospel out there. And for others, it would have been looked upon as using gospel. Be very careful of your context.

Cleveland's Gospel Workshop of America had also been building since he formed it four years earlier. *Billboard* paid attention to its September 1972 meeting at the Los Angeles Hilton, which attracted about 8,000 guests including DJs and the 50-member gospel announcers' guild.[3] Franklin also attended, and it's a safe guess what album her presence was promoting.

Still, some who had been in Franklin's inner circle within the church were not so enthused about her return to those origins for *Amazing Grace*. One of those detractors was Herbert Pickard, who kept playing only within the church ever since he accompanied C. L. Franklin:

> *Amazing Grace* was nice, but she had moved from her roots to way out there. Let me just say I liked it, I'm glad she got a chance to do it. But I was a little

[3] "National Black Gospel Meet Draws 8,000; DJs Active," *Billboard*, September 2, 1972, 1.

> prejudiced because she waited to late too try to make us think she was on a gospel kick. Back in the day, we had a fine line and it was going to be either/or. There wasn't going to be an in between. And it became an in between that left me a little wondering what's going on around here. She had left gospel music as far as I was concerned. Now here she comes with a gospel album. But it probably did a lot of good simply because she did it. There were some, I'm sure, who heard gospel music because it was Aretha and might not have listened to it had it not been Aretha. So for that I give her credit. But she wasn't ours anymore. She came back by, just stopping by. She wasn't as committed to gospel as many others were, so she lost a few points because of it. But she sang it well. You know she sang the hell out of the album. She did a good thing for gospel by doing that album, but I wouldn't be the one to say I was happy about it. It was too late.

At the time, the black and white music media enthused about the album, and if reporters and reviewers were aware of such different perspectives among Atlantic publicists or within the church, that all seemed kept in the background.

Among the mainstream American rock press, *Rolling Stone* covered *Amazing Grace* extensively at the time of its release. Along with Bob Chorush's news report in the magazine, Jon Landau reviewed the album in its August 3, 1972 issue. He enthused that "her performance is a virtuoso display of gospel pyrotechnics, done with control and imagination" and also applauded the "comprehensiveness and depth of the arrangement." Landau also put Franklin's gospel return in a wider context. He argues that *Amazing Grace* becomes a personal revitalization of the genre because of Cleveland, the band's musical sophistication, and the lead singer's own years spent in what Hamilton called "out there."

"Their music lacks the sectarian quality, the lack of ornamentation, the simplicity of the older recordings," Landau wrote. "But these qualities are made up for with a new set of virtues generated out of the horizons of Aretha's vision, the sheer, unending size of it."

Not that the consensus was unanimous among white rock journalists. Robert Christgau took a dismissive tone toward Franklin's gospel repertoire when he reviewed *Amazing Grace* in his long-running "Consumer Guide" column, which primarily ran in the *Village Voice*. "There's a purity and a passion to this church-recorded double-LP that I've missed in Aretha," he writes, "but I still find that the subdued rhythm section and pervasive call-and-response conveys more aimlessness than inspiration. Or maybe I just trust her gift of faith more readily when it's transposed to the secular realm." He grades the album a B+.[4]

Throughout the black media, *Amazing Grace* received rapturous applause. The cover story in *Soul* about the sessions was the first, as it ran about a month after the album was recorded. Linda Holmes declared in the *New York Amsterdam News* that, "All Black folks must wade their feet in Aretha's waters."[5] An array of the era's publications, like *Black Stars*, published a major photo spread and raved about the album ("there has never been a finer gospel performance by a gospel singer," Charles L. Sanders wrote). Phyl Garland's unqualified praise of the album in the October 1972 issue of *Ebony* was part of a larger article in which she echoes the sentiment that the songs from Baptist and Sanctified churches were the last vestiges of a distinctive black culture. It's essentially the same argument that ethnomusicologists such as Pearl Williams-Jones would make a few years later. "Now that the Japanese dig jazz, the British are singing the blues and white America has claimed black-derived rock as its property, gospel music must stand as one of the few remaining bastions of stone

[4] Robert Christgau, *Rock Albums of the '70s: A Critical Guide* (New York: Da Capo Press, 1981), 140–141.
[5] Linda Holmes, "Amazing Aretha Does it Again," *New York Amsterdam News*, July 8, 1972, D1.

soul folk," Garland writes. Still, during the spring and summer of 1972, the black press also took note of how the wider media started to latch onto *Amazing Grace*. *Jet* noted "how even the white rock stations are playing many of the cuts from the album which has already sold 250,000 copies, as consistently as black stations that have regular gospel programs."[6]

A British review of *Amazing Grace* wondered whether African American church music could crossover to a wider audience across the Atlantic. David Nathan, writing in the September 8–21, 1972 issue of *Blues & Soul*, has always been Franklin's biggest booster in the U.K., and would go on to write the liner notes to the 1999 Rhino reissue. His mostly laudatory review, under the headline "Aretha: Still the Queen," also considers the album a "brave experiment in attempting to bring gospel to the many thousands who either have never listened to it — or simply don't dig it." He goes further to state that, "while people can relate to soul music because its lyrics can be identified with, gospel tends to be alien to British ears." [7]

Almost 40 years later, Nathan said that his own subsequent years in the U.S.A. and experiencing

[6] "People are Talking About," *Jet*, August 24, 1972, 36.
[7] David Nathan, "Aretha: Still the Queen," *Blues & Soul*, September 8–21, 1972, 18.

American gospel first-hand in black churches made him appreciate the album even more. But he believes that British audiences haven't changed in their response, or lack thereof, to gospel even with this album's success. Nathan adds that the black religious traditions within the U.K. — especially from Caribbean and African communities — are not the same as Baptist and Sanctified traditions in the U.S.A. — Franklin's Afrocentric textiles and Barbados vacation photos notwithstanding.

But while *Amazing Grace* was being recorded, its development and fortunes seemed indirectly intertwined with the Britain-born Rolling Stones who were in the process of their distribution deal with Atlantic's Atco for their own label (Rolling Stone Records). As Franklin sang on the second night of the *Amazing Grace* recordings, Mick Jagger and Charlie Watts were in the back pews. They're visible in the film — the singer, more than the drummer as, no surprise, he's more eager to stand up and dance. At the time, the Rolling Stones would have been in Los Angeles putting the finishing mixes on *Exile on Main Street*. Neither Franklin nor the Rolling Stones' 1972 albums became known for hit singles. Gospel remains a palpable ingredient in the Stones' mashup of American influences spread throughout their career, especially on this double-album, particularly "I Just

Want to See His Face," "Let it Loose," and "Shine a Light," which included Billy Preston on organ. Yet while the Rolling Stones may have been inspired through visiting the New Temple Missionary Baptist Church, Cleveland would probably have had issues with Jagger's diction.

Slowly, after *Amazing Grace* slipped under the media radar of oldies radio formats, film and commercial soundtracks, the sales continued among the faithful. The Recording Industry Association of America (RIAA) certified it double platinum (two million copies sold) on August 26, 1992.[8]

"Aretha never had a platinum album with us, believe it or not, but this album went double platinum in the '90s," Wexler reflected to Elliott nearly 35 years after recording it. "I'm looking at my copy on the wall now. How do you like this Jewish atheist being connected with two of the best gospel recordings of our era? That one and Bob Dylan's *Slow Train Coming*."

Yet there was another American icon whose early '70s recordings provide a look as to how the gospel audience remained segregated, particularly that division within the Recording Academy's awards. Franklin won the 1972 best soul gospel performance

[8] riaa.com

Grammy for *Amazing Grace*, while Elvis Presley took home the best inspirational performance prize for *He Touched Me*. A meeting between these two icons at the awards could've served as an integrating bridge, but, apparently, it never happened.

While Franklin clearly felt strongly about *Amazing Grace*, a television appearance on April 14, 1973 reaffirms what Harris said about how reluctant she was to talk about it less than a year after its release. The singer appeared on the famous black teen-oriented dance show "Soul Train," and during a brief question-and-answer period with the young audience, she's asked if she "still has anything to do with" church singing. Franklin simply responds by just saying she does when she gets the chance. Its host Don Cornelius then brings up the question, "Wasn't the *Amazing Grace* album recorded in a church?" And Franklin just replies, "That's right. In a church right here."[9]

[9] *The Best of Soul Train* [DVD] (Time/Life, 2010).

Chapter Twelve

Richard Smallwood had just graduated from Howard with the gospel battles he fought at the university behind him when *Amazing Grace* came out in the summer of 1972. His friends in Cleveland's choir had invited him to the sessions, and he's still kicking himself that he couldn't attend. But it was enough for him to see and hear the finished album to realize that his own contentious skirmishes with the university's administration were worthwhile. In a variation on Hamilton's theme, he felt Franklin's status lent the album even more religious force. Smallwood elaborated:

> Even in the whole secular arena, you knew a lot of secular artists came out of the church, but there were very few who owned up to it, and very few who sang it. And here was somebody as great as Aretha Franklin,

> the Queen of Soul, number one r&b vocalist in the world, to come out and say, "Yes, I sing secular, but I honor gospel, as well." Church folks know she sings secular, but they want to hear her sing gospel. I remember going to Aretha's concerts in early/mid '70s and half of the place in Washington, D.C., would be full of church people I knew. I was like, "I cannot believe that she's here." Something about Aretha, always able to transcend that division between secular and sacred. When she did that project, it substantiated gospel as something that was true, something pure, something that was an art form. It encouraged me to pursue gospel even more as a career.

While *Amazing Grace* crossed those divides, the division between traditional and what's now known as contemporary gospel began at that time, and has lasted up to the present day. In some ways, the album addressed those emerging splits. But Franklin and Cleveland also presented the last resolute affirmation of the world that had been constructed years earlier. A combination of old church songs, gospel hits from Franklin's childhood, contemporary pop brushed up alongside recent religious compositions. Longstanding traditions of solo and choir singing became revamped with sophisticated arrangements and instrumentalists, and that's become the sound of the current group of gospel performers such as Smokie Norful, Vanessa Bell Armstrong, and VaShawn Mitchell.

If the album also seems like an elegy, timing shaped that narrative. Two weeks after the recording sessions, Mahalia Jackson died and Franklin sang "Precious Lord" at her Chicago funeral. The following year, in Philadelphia, she performed the same duty for Clara Ward. As Nick Salvatore writes in C. L. Franklin's biography, the minister's voice and authority had diminished by the early '70s and in June 1979, gunshots from home burglars left him in a coma until his death in 1984.

Mark Anthony Neal takes a broad view of that idea of transition, mentioning that the album's sense of nostalgia "is premised on the passing of an era in black public life." He adds, "Franklin's tribute to the black church, in an era when its influence was diminishing, celebrated its extraordinary role in building communities of cultural and political resistance and recovery."[1] Even if Franklin didn't address those issues directly as Curtis Mayfield did.

Still, what Franklin said, or inferred, through calling for collective action ("Wholy Holy") and communal achievement ("Climbing Higher Mountains"), reflected the ability of the black church to still get over,

[1] Neal, 81–83.

even during Nixon's presidency. Lincoln and Mamiya state, "as the primary social and cultural institution, the Black Church tradition is deeply embedded in black culture in general so that the sphere of politics in the African American community cannot be easily separated from it."[2] A case study they cite is the pastoral endorsement of legislators who were members of the Congressional Black Caucus.[3] To bring it all back home, caucus co-founder Rep. John Conyers, Jr. received a big dose of support in his own first election bid from Rev. C. L. Franklin.[4] Meanwhile, Lincoln and Mamiya added that (by 1990) Pentecostals had no longer been rejected as a cult, but became "a full-fledged member of the National Council of Churches and is probably that body's fastest growing constituency." Cleveland demonstrated a Sanctified beat in a Baptist church on *Amazing Grace*, but 18 years later, he wouldn't have felt as much need to verbalize it.

Meanwhile, classic gospel maintained its presence, even with the passing of such giants as Jackson and Ward. Other prominent church singers who were part of the generations that had influenced Franklin had kept recording — such as Bessie Griffin and

---

[2] Lincoln and Mamiya, 234.
[3] Lincoln and Mamiya, 216.
[4] Salvatore, 265–266.

Marion Williams — even if they were usually on such specialized labels as Malaco and Heilbut's Spirit Feel. Scores of lesser-known church artists followed the Franklin–Cleveland formula, like The Beautiful Zion Choir, who augmented *I'll Make it All Righ*t in 1973 with bassist Louis Satterfield, who co-founded Earth, Wind and Fire. Classic gospel permeated throughout American culture beyond just music production, like George Nierenberg's heralded 1982 documentary film *Say Amen, Somebody*. Six years after *Amazing Grace*, James Baldwin released his novel *Just Above My Head*, which centered around the family, life, and death of fictional gospel singer Arthur Montana. Even if the book does read as an elegy for earlier decades, its narrator (Montana's brother Hall) gives a shout-out to Cleveland.

Cleveland was also responsible for a structural transformation of gospel music that has lasted to this day. Around the time that *Amazing Grace* was released, California's popular Andraé Crouch & The Disciples' unveiled such albums as *Keep On Singin'* (Light). Crouch, who received Cleveland's endorsement in the '60s, moved away from recording the traditional songs of Dorsey and Brewster, toward his own compositions, which drew as much from pop hooks and jazz chords as they did from the blues base inherent in traditional gospel. His vocal tone's sweetness — as opposed to the rougher growls of older artists — may have also accounted for his substantial white following. And Crouch's lyrical emphasis focused on personal affirmations rather than communal movement — considerable "I" in song titles, hardly any "we" or "our." Then again, as James H. Cone wrote, even just asserting a personal identity can be a source of defiance. Smallwood would take a singular direction, as he blended Cleveland and Franklin's example with his classical training and larger choir experience to such widely popular gospel albums as *Testimony* (Sparrow) in 1992.

Cleveland's format of a large, dexterous choir using its honed cohesion to back a popular female soloist became the norm in gospel after *Amazing Grace*. One example would be the Georgia Mass Choir backing Whitney Houston on the soundtrack to *The Preacher's Wife*. Not that everyone was thrilled with how Cleveland and his followers took gospel away from its roots. In writing about Cleveland and the Ella Mitchell Singers' performance of "Deep Down in My Heart" on the CD/DVD collection *How Sweet it Was*, producer Heilbut grudgingly gives him props, saying, "I'm not completely fond of the changes he sponsored; I'd even contend that the Golden Age of soloists, groups, and quartets died on his watch, undone by the choir sound identified with him. But the evolution was organic; if anyone had the credentials to kill his parents it was [Dorsey's] Pilgrim Baptist Church's favorite son."

Still, the decline in acoustic pianos and organs in gospel has been lamented among musicians.

"When you look at Cleveland at the peak of his piano playing, on *Amazing Grace*, it's true virtuosity in terms of getting a sound out of a piano," said Eric Reed who turned his early background in the church into considerable accomplishment as a jazz pianist. He continued:

> Those intros, specifically on "God Will Take Care of You" and "Precious Memories," you hear the echoes of the barrelhouse piano. He's tugging at people's emotions, and playing the essence of real piano playing, not just gospel. He's almost the Hank Jones of gospel. With today's gospel musicians, so much of the sound is dependent on what is being plugged in. The idea of playing an acoustic piano is like a dinosaur. It's completely extinct in the modern church and if there is a piano, it's beat up, out of tune and it's covered. They have communion on it, or whatever."

Amazing Grace also stands as a coda to Franklin's key collaborative years with the producers, musicians, and arrangers at Atlantic. In 1973, she released *Hey Now Hey (The Other Side of the Sky)*, a co-production with Quincy Jones. The jazz-inspired album, with such guest instrumentalists as saxophonist Phil Woods, was recorded in Los Angeles, and was a move away from Wexler. She and her previous team with Wexler got together again in 1974 for *Let Me in Your Life*, which featured Mardin's arrangements, and Dupree, Rainey, and Purdie on most tracks. She recorded with different musicians on six more albums for the label with inconsistent results: sounding lively voicing Mayfield's songs (*Sparkle*, *Almighty Fire*), yet not so convincing chasing the decade's disco trends (*La Diva*). By the beginning of the '80s, Franklin had left the label for Arista.

Throughout Franklin's artistic and personal highs and lows in the years since that move, she remained tied to gospel. Three years after her father's death, she returned to the family's New Bethel Baptist Church to record, and serve as sole producer, on *One Lord, One Faith, One Baptism*. While *Amazing Grace* captured the passing of the traditional sound, this was a stab at reclaiming it. Three of the tracks were from the Clara Ward songbook, and Franklin brought in her sisters, including Carolyn a year before her death. Quartet singer Joe Ligon was onboard, as was Mavis Staples to reinterpret "Oh Happy Day." With so many guest appearances — including lengthy sermons from Jesse Jackson — Franklin didn't provide enough room for herself to reach higher and longer as she had 15 years earlier.

Still, Franklin remained loyal to the venerable gospel sound. *One Lord* became her sole Dove Award from the Gospel Music Association in the category of "traditional gospel album of the year," which, its web site reminds, was formerly known as "traditional black gospel." She'd go on to nab a Grammy that year, this time the category was called "best soul gospel performance, female."

A few years later, gospel became big business — following the organizational model that Cleveland and Wexler had envisioned and planned. Shawn E. Rhea described this movement in the July 1998 issue of *Black Enterprise* in terms that already conjure nostalgia from when there actually was some power in the record industry. Just as Atlantic had formed Cotillion to jump into the gospel market in the late '60s, it launched Pioneer to do the same almost 30 years later. But the numbers were more firm in the mid '90s, as SoundScan started to track sales in the genre. Rhea reported that, "a 1996 report by the Recording Industry of America showed earnings of $538 million, up from $381 million in 1995, a 41 percent jump."[5] Nowadays,

[5] Shawn E. Rhea, "Gospel Rises Again," *Black Enterprise*, July 1998, 95.

with the ascendancy of quality home recording and digital downloads, maybe there will be a resurgence of individualistic gospel albums recorded live in small and medium-size churches — showing another side of the ostensibly homegrown influence of *Amazing Grace*.

Cleveland didn't live to see the realization of this industry that he had envisioned. He died in 1991. Archbishop Carl Bean hosted a salute to him in Los Angeles in the late '80s:

> He got sicker and sicker and wound up with a hole in the throat, I think it was a tracheotomy. I don't think it was from AIDS. I think it was from his years of cigarette smoke. So near the end of his life, the gospel community rallied around him and came to salute him. The Caravans reunited, Soul Stirrers, Clouds of Joy, all of us went. It was one of the hardest nights of my life. He wanted to say something, and all he could say was "thank you," and when he stuck his hand in that hole, all of us just lost it. Here was a guy who made his living from his voice, and he couldn't use it.

The core *Amazing Grace* rhythm team of Purdie, Rainey and Dupree recorded and toured off and on with Franklin, but they were never a full-time team with her for much longer after that album. They weren't hungry for work, as each of them — together or separate — have constantly been involved with a wide range of gigs. Among his 2,500 sessions, Dupree played on Donny Hathaway's sensational *Live* and co-led the instrumental funk band Stuff. He died of emphysema at his home in Fort Worth, Texas, on May 8, 2011 at the age of 68.

Rainey sat in the bass chair for Steely Dan's 1970s megahit albums and on the theme to "Sanford And Son," a television sitcom set in Watts. Purdie also recorded with Steely Dan and on numerous other rock and jazz sessions. Each of them continues to perform and lead musical clinics and workshops worldwide. Throughout the years, they continued performing with such gospel groups as The Clark Sisters and Staple Singers.

"A reason why I worked with so many different gospel groups was because of *Amazing Grace*," Purdie said. "They thought I only did gospel."

Although not as visible, most of the *Amazing Grace* crew have kept up rewarding careers. Gene Paul is a highly respected engineer, currently with G&J Audio in Union City, N.J., where he specializes in high-end mastering and Pro Tools mixing. Hamilton directs the Voices of Inspiration Community Choir in Compton, California, and is pastor of the city's Community Missionary Baptist Church, which serves its neighborhood in multiple ways. During my visit to interview him, he was also running a clothing drive in the church's front yard while assembling information on prostate cancer awareness. The New Temple Missionary Baptist Church also has its own choir and conducts necessary charity work in Watts. There is no cornerstone, plaque or other marker on or near the church that designates the recording: Such would be inappropriate for a house of worship, anyway. But George Ashford said every so often people — usually from other countries — come in and ask questions about *Amazing Grace.*

Lupper never fulfilled the promise that Hamilton and so many others saw in him. His only album as leader, 1975's *Testify* (Creed), just showed flashes of what made his reputation as a keyboardist. He died of unknown causes on July 20, 1980, about a month before his twenty-seventh birthday.[6]

Franklin herself keeps returning to religious music, if not as visibly as in earlier years. And nowadays she's become more an elder pop celebrity rather than cultural symbol. She's headlined revivals, like at Detroit's Greater Emmanuel Institutional Church of God in Christ in June 2007. In an instance of either making sure what goes around comes around, or the ties that still bind gospel families, her touring

---

[6] State of California, California Death Index, 1940–1997. Sacramento, CA, State of California Department of Health Services, Center for Health Statistics.

pianist has been Richard Gibbs, the son of Caravan Inez Andrews, who admired Franklin as a gospel baby in the '50s. Smallwood finally got his chance to work alongside her when she recruited his group to perform songs from *Amazing Grace*, as well as *One Lord*, in Madison Square Garden in June 2005. The musical and commercial interweaving, which had been reported in *Black Enterprise*, took on a clear dimension for this concert. The event was billed as McDonald's Gospelfest, which Jon Pareles in *The New York Times* described as "an uncommon association of fast-food and virtue."[7] Still, for the musicians, the corporate logos, even the environment itself, were not the primary concern.

"The excitement in the building was incredible, it was a very hot spell and Aretha doesn't do air conditioning," Smallwood said about the singer who's notorious for believing that such forced ventilation harms her throat. "So every vent had to be covered, every piece of air conditioning had to be turned off. It was like a sauna. We were drenched, but nobody cared. We were there to experience this amazing journey. Anybody else we'd complain, but it was

[7]Jon Pareles, "Respect, but this Time Delivering it to a Higher Power," *The New York Times*, June 6, 2005, E5.

Aretha, so who cares? Made me feel even closer to what she's done her whole life."

In the media push before the Madison Square Garden event, Franklin mentioned her allegiance to the traditional sounds that she spent her own childhood performing. The *New York Amsterdam News* quoted her as saying that she, "likes some of what's considered gospel music today, but finds much of it, 'a little too finger-popping boogying for me to be gospel.'"[8]

She's not alone, and her traditional emphasis helps account for the continuing magic of *Amazing Grace*. More important than the two million copies sold, the impact on the countless gospel singers throughout the country has endured. Some are well known like Smokie Norful who visits her moans on his own concert recording, *Smokie Norful Live* (EMI). Singer and music minister VaShawn Mitchell, born in 1976, adds that the story of *Amazing Grace* remains as important to him as those songs:

> As I researched Aretha and C. L. and James Cleveland, their whole story was an inspiration for what I do. Just how people connect, collaborate and meet each other.

---

[8] Matt Rogers, "Back to Gospel Roots for Queen of Soul," *New York Amsterdam News*, June 9, 2005, 19.

Other recent traditional gospel singers who've begun charting their paths in the decades since *Amazing Grace* are not yet as well known. One is Donna Gay, a strong Chicago vocalist and the niece of the Gay Sisters, whose "God Will Take Care of You" inspired Franklin more than 50 years ago. Another Chicagoan, Debbie Orange, released her debut, *Debbie Orange Sings Church Live* (Safety Zone) in 2010. Like Franklin's double-album, Orange recorded hers in front of a choir (St. John's Missionary Baptist on Chicago's South Side). Orange also bridged the different denominations throughout her life. She grew up Pentecostal in the '70s, yet became a Baptist in the '80s, particularly because the strict Sanctified parishioners felt her natural singing style was too bluesy: similar to Franklin's. Orange also shares Franklin's reservations about what's considered contemporary Christian music, and feels that a currently popular form called praise and worship puts too much emphasis on elegant ballads and pretty notes. What's crucial is to preserve the feeling and legacy of the songs that brought Aretha Franklin into the New Temple Missionary Baptist Church in January 1972.

"I always look for 'Amazing Grace' and 'How I Got Over' when I go into a church," Orange said. "Just like my mom taught me those old songs, we have to pass them on. That's Aretha Franklin and James Cleveland's legacy. I pray their songs will never die."

As Wexler talked about his work on *Amazing Grace* with Alan Elliott a year before the end of his life in 2008, the team's entire legacy, and mortality, sounded like they were on his mind, too. They had been discussing the film when Elliott asked Wexler if he and Franklin could have some sort of personal reconciliation, just considering all of their great work together. Wexler surprised him to say that it already happened, and that it was the notoriously quiet, seemingly recalcitrant, Franklin who made the first move.

"Aretha called me a couple weeks ago," Wexler said. "It was a half hour of love and nostalgia for the first time in I don't know how many decades."

Sources

Books/Articles

James Abbington (ed.). *Readings in African American Church Music and Worship* (Chicago: GIA Publications, 2001).

Vince Aletti. "Aretha and the Ladies' Soul." *Creem*; May 1972, 59–60.

"Aretha and Rev. Cleveland Record 'Precious Memories'." *Black Stars*; April 1972, 63.

Michael Awkward. *Soul Covers: Rhythm and Blues Remakes and the Struggle for Artistic Identity* (Durham, N.C.: Duke University Press, 2007).

James Baldwin. *Go Tell it on the Mountain* (New York, Dial Press/Random House, 1952).

James Baldwin. *Just Above My Head* (New York: Dial Press/Random House, 1979).

Mark Bego. *Aretha Franklin: The Queen of Soul* (New York: Da Capo, 2001).

Mary J. Blige. "Aretha Franklin." *Rolling Stone*; November 27, 2008, 73.

Horace Clarence Boyer. "An Overview: Gospel Music Comes of Age." *Black World*: (November 1973), 42–86.

Horace Clarence Boyer. "Gospel Music." *Music Educators Journal*; Vol. 64, no. 9 (May 1978), 34–43.

Horace Clarence Boyer. "Contemporary Gospel Music." *The Black Perspective in Music*; Vol. 7, no. 1 (Spring 1979), 5–58.

Daphne A. Brooks. "Bold Soul Ingenue." Liner notes to *Take a Look: Aretha Franklin Complete On Columbia* (Sony/Legacy), 2011.

Mellonnee Burim. "Gospel Music: Review of the Literature." *Music Educators Journal*; Vol. 69, no. 9 (May 1983), 58–61.

Jon Burlingame. "'Grace' Film Finally Near." *Variety*; January 7, 2010. (www.variety.com).

Walter Price Burrell. "A Personal Look at Aretha Franklin." *Black Stars*; (June 1972), 6–15.

Bil Carpenter. *Uncloudy Days: The Gospel Music Encyclopedia* (San Francisco, CA.: Backbeat Books, 2005).

Bob Chorush. "Aretha Sings in a Church in Watts." *Rolling Stone*; April 13, 1972, 22.

Robert Christgau. *Rock Albums of the '70s: A Critical Guide* (New York: Da Capo Press, 1981).

James H. Cone. *The Spirituals and the Blues* (Seabury Press, 1972; 3rd Printing, Maryknoll, N.Y.: Orbis Books, 1995).

Robert Darden. *People Get Ready: A New History of Black Gospel Music* (New York: Continuum, 2004).

Jacqueline Cogdell DjeDje. "Gospel Music in the Los Angeles Black Community: A Historical Overview." *Black Music Research Journal*; Vol. 9, no. 1 (Spring 1989), 35–79.

Matt Dobkin. *I Never Loved a Man the Way I Love You* (New York: St. Martin's Griffin, 2004).

Tom Doyle. "Arif Mardin: Producer." *Sound on Sound*; July 2004 (www.soundonsound.com).

W. E. B. Du Bois. *The Souls of Black Folk* (New York: Penguin, 1996 edition).

David Evans. "Black Religious Music." *The Journal of American Folklore*; Vol. 86, no. 339 (January–March 1973), 82–86.

Marshall Frady. *Martin Luther King, Jr.: A Life* (New York: Penguin, 2002).

Aretha Franklin. "From Gospel to Jazz is Not Disrespect for The Lord." *New York Amsterdam News*; August 26, 1961, 17.

Aretha Franklin and David Ritz. *Aretha: From These Roots* (New York: Villard, 1999).

Reverend C. L. Franklin. *Give Me this Mountain* (Urbana, IL.: University of Illinois Press, 1989).

E. Franklin Frazier. *The Negro Church in America* (New York: Schocken Books, 1966).

Josh Alan Friedman. *Tell the Truth Until They Bleed* (San Francisco, CA.: Backbeat Books, 2008).

Will Friedwald. *A Biographical Guide to the Great Jazz and Pop Singers* (New York: Pantheon, 2010).

Phyl Garland. *The Sound of Soul* (Chicago: Henry Regnery Company, 1969).

Cheryl Townsend Gilkes. "'Together and in Harness': Women's Traditions in the Sanctified Church." *Signs*; Vol. 10, no. 4 (Summer 1985), 678–699.

Monique Guillory and Richard C. Green (eds.). *Soul: Black Power, Politics, and Pleasure* (New York: New York University Press, 1998).

Peter Guralnick. *Sweet Soul Music* (New York: Harper and Row, 1986).

Peter Guralnick. *Dream Boogie: The Triumph of Sam Cooke* (New York: Little Brown, 2005).

Michael W. Harris, *The Rise of Gospel Blues: The Music of Thomas Andrew Dorsey in the Urban Church* (New York: Oxford University Press, 1992).

Anthony Heilbut. *The Gospel Sound* (New York: Limelight Editions, 1997).

Bob Herbert. "Thinking of Aretha." *The New York Times*; December 25, 2010, A21.

Gerri Hirshey. *Nowhere to Run: The Story of Soul Music* (New York: Da Capo, 1994).

Charles Hobson. "The Gospel Truth." *DownBeat*; May 30, 1968, 16–20.

Charles Hobson. "Gospel Summit Meeting." *Black Stars*; September 1972, 62–66.

Chris Hodenfield. "Baby, I Know: Reassessing Aretha." *Rolling Stone*; May 23, 1974, 62–68.

Richard Iton. *In Search of the Black Fantastic* (New York: Oxford University Press, 2008).

Jerma A. Jackson. *Singing in My Soul: Black Gospel Music in a Secular Age* (Chapel Hill, N.C., University of North Carolina Press, 2004).

Irene Jackson-Brown. "Developments in Black Gospel Performance and Scholarship." *Black Music Research Journal*; Vol. 10, no. 1 (Spring 1990), 36–42.

Jon Landau. "Aretha Hits Note After Note I Always Knew Was There but Never Heard." *Rolling Stone*, August 3, 1972, 36.

Andrew Legg. "A Taxonomy of Musical Gesture in African American Gospel Music." *Popular Music*; Vol. 29/1 (2010), 103–129.

Lawrence W. Levine. *Black Culture and Black Consciousness* (New York: Oxford University Press, 1977).

C. Eric Lincoln and Lawrence H. Mamiya. *The Black Church in the African American Experience* (Durham, N.C.: Duke University Press, 1990).

J. Wendell Mapson, Jr. *The Ministry of Music in the Black Church* (Valley Forge, PA: Judson Press, 1984).

W. K. McNeil (ed.). *Encyclopedia of American Gospel Music* (New York: Routledge, 2005).

David Nathan. "Aretha: Still the Queen." *Blues & Soul*; September 8–21, 1972, 18.

Mark Anthony Neal. *What the Music Said: Black Popular Music and Black Public Culture* (New York: Routledge, 1999).

Platon. "Portfolio: The Promise." *The New Yorker*; February 15 & 22, 2010, 94–115.

Dunstan Prial. *The Producer: John Hammond and the Soul of American Music* (New York: Farrar, Straus and Giroux, 2006).

Guthrie P. Ramsey, Jr., *Race Music* (Berkeley, CA.: University of California Press, 2004).

Bernice Johnson Reagon (ed.). *We'll Understand It Better By and By: Pioneering African American Gospel Performers* (Washington, D.C.: Smithsonian, 1992).

Teresa L. Reed. *The Holy Profane: Religion in Black Popular Music* (Lexington, KY.: University Press of Kentucky, 2003).

Johannes Riedel. *Soul Music Black & White: The Influence of Black Music on the Churches* (Minneapolis, MN: Augsburg Publishing House, 1975).

Nick Salvatore. *Singing in a Strange Land: C. L. Franklin, the Black Church, and the Transformation of America* (New York: Little Brown, 2005).

Charles L. Sanders. "On Records." *Black Stars*; August, 1972, 74.

R. J. Smith. *The Great Black Way: L.A. in the 1940s and the Lost African American Renaissance* (New York: Public Affairs, 2006).

Judy Spiegelman. "After Ten Years Aretha Brings it all Back Home." *Soul*; February 28, 1972, 1–5.

M. Cordell Thompson. "Aretha is Rocking Steady Now." *Jet*; March 9, 1972, 59–63.

Steve Turner. *Amazing Grace: The Story of America's Most Beloved Song* (New York: Ecco, 2002).

Wyatt Tee Walker. *"Somebody's Calling My Name": Black Sacred Music and Social Change* (Valley Forge, PA.: Judson Press, 1979).

Brian Ward. *Just My Soul Responding* (Berkeley, CA.: University of California Press, 1998).

Willa Ward-Royster and Toni Rose. *How I Got Over: Clara Ward and the World-Famous Ward Singers* (Philadelphia, PA.: Temple University Press, 1997).

Melinda E. Weekes. "This House, this Music: Exploring the Interdependent Interpretive Relationship Between the

Contemporary Black Church and Contemporary Gospel Music." *Black Music Research Journal*; Vol. 25, nos. 1–2 (Spring–Fall 2005), 43–72.

Bernard Weinraub. "Aretha, So Damn Happy About Her New Album." *The New York Times*; September 28, 2003, A27.

Pete Welding. "Focus on Aretha Franklin." *DownBeat*; September 28, 1961, 18.

Craig Werner. *Higher Ground: Stevie Wonder, Aretha Franklin, Curtis Mayfield and the Rise and Fall of American Soul* (New York: Crown, 2005).

Craig Werner. *A Change is Gonna Come: Music, Race & the Soul of America* (Ann Arbor, MI.: University of Michigan Press, 2006).

Jerry Wexler and David Ritz. *Rhythm and the Blues: A Life in American Music* (New York: Alfred A. Knopf, 1993).

Pearl Williams-Jones. "Afro-American Gospel Music: A Crystallization of the Black Aesthetic." *Ethnomusicology*; Vol. 19, no. 3 (September 1975), 373–385.

Valerie Wilmer. "Aretha ... Lady Soul." *DownBeat*; August 8, 1968, 16.

Josephine Wright. "A Preliminary Bibliographical Guide to Periodical Literature for Black Music Research." *Black Music Research Journal*; Vol. 10, no. 1 (Spring 1990), 14–17.

Websites

www.blog.justmovingon.info
www.sirshambling.com
www.soul-sides.com
www.theblackgospelblog.com

Also available in the series:

1. *Dusty in Memphis* by Warren Zanes
2. *Forever Changes* by Andrew Hultkrans
3. *Harvest* by Sam Inglis
4. *The Kinks Are the Village Green Preservation Society* by Andy Miller
5. *Meat Is Murder* by Joe Pernice
6. *The Piper at the Gates of Dawn* by John Cavanagh
7. *Abba Gold* by Elisabeth Vincentelli
8. *Electric Ladyland* by John Perry
9. *Unknown Pleasures* by Chris Ott
10. *Sign 'O' the Times* by Michaelangelo Matos
11. *The Velvet Underground and Nico* by Joe Harvard
12. *Let It Be* by Steve Matteo
13. *Live at the Apollo* by Douglas Wolk
14. *Aqualung* by Allan Moore
15. *OK Computer* by Dai Griffiths
16. *Let It Be* by Colin Meloy
17. *Led Zeppelin IV* by Erik Davis
18. *Exile on Main Sreet* by Bill Janovitz
19. *Pet Sounds* by Jim Fusilli
20. *Ramones* by Nicholas Rombes
21. *Armed Forces* by Franklin Bruno
22. *Murmur* by J. Niimi
23. *Grace* by Daphne Brooks
24. *Endtroducing ...* by Eliot Wilder
25. *Kick Out the Jams* by Don McLeese
26. *Low* by Hugo Wilcken
27. *Born in the U.S.A.* by Geoffrey Himes
28. *Music from Big Pink* by John Niven
29. *In the Aeroplane Over the Sea* by Kim Cooper
30. *Paul's Boutique* by Dan LeRoy
31. *Doolittle* by Ben Sisario
32. *There's a Riot Goin' On* by Miles Marshall Lewis
33. *The Stone Roses* by Alex Green
34. *In Utero* by Gillian G. Gaar
35. *Highway 61 Revisited* by Mark Polizzotti
36. *Loveless* by Mike McGonigal
37. *The Who Sell Out* by John Dougan
38. *Bee Thousand* by Marc Woodworth
39. *Daydream Nation* by Matthew Stearns
40. *Court and Spark* by Sean Nelson
41. *Use Your Illusion Vols 1 and 2* by Eric Weisbard
42. *Songs in the Key of Life* by Zeth Lundy
43. *The Notorious Byrd Brothers* by Ric Menck
44. *Trout Mask Replica* by Kevin Courrier
45. *Double Nickels on the Dime* by Michael T. Fournier
46. *Aja* by Don Breithaupt

47. *People's Instinctive Travels and the Paths of Rhythm* by Shawn Taylor
48. *Rid of Me* by Kate Schatz
49. *Achtung Baby* by Stephen Catanzarite
50. *If You're Feeling Sinister* by Scott Plagenhoef
51. *Pink Moon* by Amanda Petrusich
52. *Let's Talk About Love* by Carl Wilson
53. *Swordfishtrombones* by David Smay
54. *20 Jazz Funk Greats* by Drew Daniel
55. *Horses* by Philip Shaw
56. *Master of Reality* by John Darnielle
57. *Reign in Blood* by D. X. Ferris
58. *Shoot Out the Lights* by Hayden Childs
59. *Gentlemen* by Bob Gendron
60. *Rum, Sodomy & the Lash* by Jeffery T. Roesgen
61. *The Gilded Palace of Sin* by Bob Proehl
62. *Pink Flag* by Wilson Neate
63. *XO* by Matthew LeMay
64. *Illmatic* by Matthew Gasteier
65. *Radio City* by Bruce Eaton
66. *One Step Beyond ...* by Terry Edwards
67. *Another Green World* by Geeta Dayal
68. *Zaireeka* by Mark Richardson
69. *69 Love Songs* by L. D. Beghtol
70. *Facing Future* by Dan Kois
71. *It Takes a Nation of Millions to Hold Us Back* by Christopher R. Weingarten
72. *Wowee Zowee* by Bryan Charles
73. *Highway to Hell* by Joe Bonomo
74. *Song Cycle* by Richard Henderson
75. *Spiderland* by Scott Tennent
76. *Kid A* by Marvin Lin
77. *Tusk* by Rob Trucks
78. *Pretty Hate Machine* by Daphne Carr
79. *Chocolate and Cheese* by Hank Shteamer
80. *American Recordings* by Tony Tost
81. *Some Girls* by Cyrus Patell
82. *You're Living All Over Me* by Nick Attfield
83. *Marquee Moon* by Bryan Waterman
84. *Amazing Grace* by Aaron Cohen
85. *Dummy* by R. J. Wheaton
86. *Fear of Music* by Jonathan Lethem
87. *Histoire de Melody Nelson* by Darran Anderson
88. *Flood* by S. Alexander Reed and Elizabeth Sandifer
89. *I Get Wet* by Phillip Crandall
90. *Selected Ambient Works Volume II* by Marc Weidenbaum
91. *Entertainment!* by Kevin J.H. Dettmar
92. *Blank Generation* by Pete Astor

93. *Donuts* by Jordan Ferguson
94. *Smile* by Luis Sanchez
95. *Definitely Maybe* by Alex Niven
96. *Exile in Guyville* by Gina Arnold
97. *My Beautiful Dark Twisted Fantasy* by Kirk Walker Graves
98. *The Grey Album* by Charles Fairchild
99. *()* by Ethan Hayden
100. *Dangerous* by Susan Fast
101. *Tago Mago* by Alan Warner
102. *Ode to Billie Joe* by Tara Murtha
103. *Live Through This* by Anwen Crawford
104. *Freedom of Choice* by Evie Nagy
105. *Fresh Fruit for Rotting Vegetables* by Michael Stewart Foley
106. *Super Mario Bros.* by Andrew Schartmann
107. *Beat Happening* by Bryan C. Parker
108. *Metallica* by David Masciotra
109. *A Live One* by Walter Holland
110. *Bitches Brew* by George Grella Jr.
111. *Parallel Lines* by Kembrew McLeod
112. *Workingman's Dead* by Buzz Poole
113. *Hangin' Tough* by Rebecca Wallwork
114. *Geto Boys* by Rolf Potts
115. *Dig Me Out* by Jovana Babovic
116. *Sound of Silver* by Ryan Leas
117. *Donny Hathaway Live* by Emily J. Lordi
118. *Psychocandy* by Paula Mejia
119. *The Modern Lovers* by Sean L. Maloney
120. *Soundtrack from Twin Peaks* by Clare Nina Norelli
121. *Colossal Youth* by Michael Blair and Joe Bucciero
122. *Bizarre Ride II the Pharcyde* by Andrew Barker
123. *The Suburbs* by Eric Eidelstein
124. *Workbook* by Walter Biggins and Daniel Couch
125. *Uptown Saturday Night* by Sean L. Maloney
126. *The Raincoats* by Jenn Pelly
127. *Homogenic* by Emily Mackay
128. *Okie from Muskogee* by Rachel Lee Rubin
129. *In on the Kill Taker* by Joe Gross
130. *24 Hour Revenge Therapy* by Ronen Givony
131. *Transformer* by Ezra Furman
132. *Siouxsie and the Banshees' Peepshow* by Samantha Bennett
133. *Drive-By Truckers' Southern Rock Opera* by Rien Fertel
134. *dc Talks' Jesus Freak* by Will Stockton and D. Gilson
135. *Tori Amos's Boys for Pele* by Amy Gentry